Haskins & Sells • Our First Seventy-Five Years

Designed by New Center, Inc.
Manufactured in the United States of America
by Crafton Graphic Company, Inc.
Library of Congress Catalog Card No. 75-132631

Foreword

This 75th Anniversary historical volume was written primarily by Arthur B. Foye with the advice, review, and concurrence of Ralph S. Johns and J. Harry Williams. We are indebted to them for the considerable time and effort which produced this valuable contribution to the Firm's historical record.

The history of a professional firm can be written only in terms of individual participation, which in a firm of the scope of Haskins & Sells would embrace the contributions of hundreds or thousands of people. Time and space would not permit complete coverage and yet the real history of our Firm was undoubtedly developed by a multitude of partners and staff in an "unnotable" performance of their professional responsibilities—"unnotable" only because their performance was in the pursuit of our Firm ideal—the pursuit of excellence.

John W. Queenan

Preface

Haskins & Sells are people. In this 75th Anniversary volume your committee would have wished it possible to describe the contributions of all of the people who have contributed to the success of the Firm but space limitations did not permit. Nevertheless the committee recognizes that the public practice of accountancy is a personal service and that the success of the Firm—past, present, and future—depends upon people.

In 1920 there was recognition of the 25th Anniversary of the founding of the Firm of Haskins & Sells. In 1935 a limited volume was published honoring the Firm's 40th Anniversary. And in 1950 another more extensive volume, written largely by George P. Auld, was published honoring the Firm's 50th Anniversary.

Committee On History
Arthur B. Foye, Chairman
Ralph S. Johns
J. Harry Williams

June 1, 1970

"The ideal conception by the profession itself of its true mission... sets it upon a platform of its own as a learned profession, self-impelled to culture, to moral enlargement, and to scientific attainment, and lays a basis of confidence for every business enterprise that in professional accountancy there is a self-centered soul of economic truth."

Charles Waldo Haskins

Table of Contents

1

*Charles Waldo Haskins—Elijah Watt Sells—
Dockery Commission Service*

When Charles Waldo Haskins and Elijah Watt Sells first met in 1893, the American public accounting profession was barely in its teens. It had come into being in the eighties at a climactic point in a period of growth and consolidation of the national economy. During the preceding twenty years, the national railway mileage had been quadrupled by the completion of the Union Pacific (in 1869) and other great trunk lines, together with scores of closely-woven regional networks. Keeping pace with the transformation of the railway map, a profusion of new industrial enterprises had sprung up in every corner of the land, many of them ill-adapted to meeting the conditions of trade on a continental or world-wide scale. A striking development was the inauguration of a period of corporate consolidations designed to effect economies through large-scale operations—a process which reached a climax in the years 1898-1902, with 168 consolidations of manufacturing and mining enterprises capitalized at 5¾ billion dollars. The complexities of the financial and cost accounting problems involved were alone sufficient to bring into existence a specialized profession competent to offer sound advice on how to deal with them; and for a period of still further expansion of production then in sight, it was apparent that the role of the accounting specialist would not diminish.

More than that, the investment banking business, organized to provide industry with the large amounts of new capital required for additions and improvements, had now assumed large proportions; and underwriters, as well as a growing body of investors, felt the need of having financial reports certified by independent auditors. Within industry the increasing weight and diversity of managerial responsibilities impelled management to look to independent auditors to establish the integrity and competence of employees who handled the assets and kept the accounts.

Charles Waldo Haskins came of a long line of American ancestors. The first Haskins to come to the United States was Robert in the early part of the eighteenth century. His son John, born in 1729, became a prominent figure in the life of Boston. At the age of eighteen he was a privateersman aboard a letter-of-marque vessel commissioned to fight against the French and Spanish, by both of whom he was taken prisoner. At the Lexington alarm in 1775 he was a Captain in the old Boston Regiment. His wife was descended from Reverend Henry Dunster, first President of Harvard, and from John Howland, one of the signers of the "Mayflower" compact. John Haskins was a prominent and successful merchant, as was his son Robert, the great-grandfather of Charles Waldo Haskins. The great-grandmother was the daughter of Reverend William Emerson, who built the "Old Manse" made famous by Hawthorne, and who died while serving as Chaplain with the American Army at Ticonderoga. She was also the aunt of Ralph Waldo Emerson. Robert's son, Thomas Waldo Haskins, was also a merchant in Boston—the largest hardware dealer in the City. Waldo Emerson Haskins, the father of Charles Waldo Haskins, was born in Roxbury, Massachusetts in 1827, and in 1851 moved to New York to engage in the banking business with his uncle, George Soren. He married Amelia Cammeyer, and moved to Brooklyn, where Charles Waldo Haskins was born on January 11, 1852, when Franklin Pierce was President of the United States. It was Pierce who supported Commodore Perry's opening of Japan to the western world in 1854. However, it was also Pierce who disapproved of the proposal in the "Ostend Manifesto" in 1854 of three American Ambassadors in Europe to purchase Cuba from Spain for $120,000,000. Charles Waldo Haskins was educated at private schools and the Brooklyn Polytechnic Institute, from which he graduated in 1867. For five years he was employed in the accounting department of Frederick Butterfield & Company, a New York importing firm. He later spent two years studying art in Paris. After returning home, he was employed for a while in the brokerage office of his father, Waldo Emerson Haskins, and thereafter joined the accounting department of the North River Construction Company, then building the New York, West Shore and Buffalo Railway. Upon completion of the line, he

Charles Waldo Haskins, founding partner of the Firm and first Dean of New York University's School of Commerce, Accounts and Finance. "His eyes were turned to the future, not to the past."

became its general bookkeeper and auditor of disbursements, continuing in this work until the New York Central acquired the road in 1886. He then began the public practice of accountancy in New York City. At that time at the age of 33 he married Miss Henrietta Havemeyer, a daughter of Albert Havemeyer, a leading citizen and merchant in New York and of the family so well known in the financial and social history of the City. Mrs. Haskins' uncle, the Honorable William F. Havemeyer, was New York's most popular Mayor and was twice the incumbent of that office. Naturally, the connections of the Havemeyer family supplementing the connections of his father in the brokerage and banking world were of great assistance in Mr. Haskins' budding practice.

During the next seven years, Mr. Haskins held, incident to his professional work, the offices of Secretary of the Manhattan Trust Company and Secretary of the Old Dominion Construction Company, as well as appointments as Comptroller of the Central of Georgia Railway, Comptroller of the Ocean Steamship Company, Comptroller of the Chesapeake & Western Railroad, and Receiver of the Augusta Mining and Investment Company.

He took an active interest in the passage, by the New York Legislature in 1896, of an Act to Regulate the Profession of Public Accountancy which was the first legislation in the Country to create the professional designation "Certified Public Accountant." Mr. Haskins qualified under the terms of the Act and was chosen the first President of the Board of State Examiners of Public Accountants instituted thereunder.

The following year he was elected President of the New York State Society of Certified Public Accountants, an office which he held until his death in 1903. He took a leading part in the founding in 1900 of the School of Commerce, Accounts and Finance of New York University. As its first Dean he set his sights high and imparted a strong initial impetus to a school which was to make a notable contribution to establishing public accountancy on the plane of a profession. The University in June 1902 conferred upon him the honorary degree of Master of Humane Letters.

Mr. Haskins was a man of warm and robust personality and of varied gifts and interests. His scholarly and artistic aptitudes were well developed, he was a clear and convincing writer and lecturer, and an active worker for good government. In the field of his major interest he exhibited a strong sense of the mission of the public accountant in advancing the cause of truth in accounts and thereby aiding in a sound expansion of the national economy. At the unveiling of a tablet erected to his memory at New York University in 1919 a tribute was paid to his qualities by Hon. Frank A. Vanderlip in these words: "Two features of his character stand out most clearly before me as I look back on the man and his work. First, he was filled with unselfish professional zeal; second, his eyes were turned to the future, not the past."

The family of Elijah Watt Sells goes far back into American history as his great-grandfather, John Sells, served in the Revolutionary War as a private in the Pennsylvania Militia.

Elijah Watt Sells was born in Muscatine, Iowa on March 1, 1858. His father, Elijah Sells, was at various times Secretary of State for Iowa and was Auditor of the Post Office for the Treasury Department under Abraham Lincoln. In the late eighteen sixties Elijah Sells was appointed Indian Agent with headquarters at Baldwin, Kansas. His son, Elijah Watt Sells, started in Baker University in Baldwin, Kansas, but left in 1873 when he was 16 to become assistant station agent at Gardiner, Kansas for the Leavenworth, Lawrence & Galveston Railroad, later part of the Santa Fe System. Fortunately or unfortunately, the man in charge of the office had serious lapses and Sells, despite his youth, carried the burden of the office, rendering careful and accurate reports. This came to the attention of the Home Office through a visit of an inspector and a position followed under George H. Nettleton in the General Office of the Kansas City, Fort Scott & Memphis Railroad. He remained with divisions of the Chicago, Burlington & Quincy System until 1879. Then followed fourteen years of accounting experience with railroads in various parts of the country.

1879-1881 Cashier, Paymaster and Bookkeeper for the Chicago, Clinton, Dubuque & Minnesota Railroad in Dubuque, Iowa. (It was in Dubuque that he met Miss Mabel Graves, whom he married in 1884.)

1881-1884 Chief Clerk for Comptroller, Oregon Railway and Navigation Company, Portland, Oregon.

1884 Auditor—Pacific Coast Railway, San Luis Obispo, California.

1884-1887 Auditor—Oregon Improvement Company, San Francisco, California.

Elijah Watt Sells, founding partner of the Firm, standing at his desk. His exceptional qualities of mind and heart brought him the respect and affection of his associates.

1887-1888—Back to the Kansas City, Fort Scott & Memphis Railroad—the one in which he started—now as Assistant Comptroller.

1888-1893—Secretary and Auditor—The Colorado Midland Railway Company, part of Atchison, Topeka & Santa Fe System. In May 1893 he was transferred to Chicago to be Chief Clerk for the General Auditor of the Atchison, Topeka & Santa Fe Railroad. Here he came under the eye of J. W. Reinhart, the President of the Santa Fe. Reinhart had come up through all the grades of railroad employment and management, starting twenty years before as a clerk for the superintendent of construction of the Pennsylvania Railroad at a salary of $10.00 a month. In 1893 at the age of 42, Reinhart was President of the Santa Fe.

In 1896 Mr. Sells became a Certified Public Accountant of New York under the provisions of the State law enacted that year, later qualifying under similar laws of eight other states and becoming a member of the professional societies of several of them. He was for two terms, 1906 and 1907, president of the American Association of Public Accountants. He was active in the organization of the American Institute of Accountants, and served at different times as member of its Council and its Executive Committee.

Mr. Sells was deeply interested in the advancing of professional education, and with his partner and others participated in the founding of the School of Commerce, Accounts and Finance of New York University. In 1924, before his death, there was established by a number of his friends in the American Institute of Accountants a fund for annual awards for the candidates attaining the highest standing in CPA examinations throughout the Country. Shortly after his death, his sister, Mrs. John H. Bovard, founded at New York University a scholarship in his memory. An early advocate of publicity of corporation accounts, he lived to see it recognized as one of the pillars of a healthy industrial society. In an address in 1911 he said: "Full publicity of the affairs of corporations would be beneficial not only to the public but to the corporations themselves, as the actions and investigations brought about by the public uneasiness would be largely forestalled thereby...."

Among the papers of his authorship on professional subjects were "Corporate Management Compared with Government Control"; "Cost Accounting for Agricultural Implements and Vehicle Manufacturers"; "Publicity of Financial Affairs of Corporations"; "The Natural Business Year"; "The Accounting Profession—Its Demands and Its Future."

He knew well the value of recreation and of peaceful interludes in life. In the year before Mr. Haskins died, Mr. Sells bought a rugged rundown farm in northern Westchester County, thirty-five miles from New York. "It was a spread of marsh and rocks interspersed with lean, small fields and mowing lots, enclosed by toppling stone walls and unkempt wire fences. There was scarcely an outbuilding worthy of the name. The house, though staunchly built, was cramped; moreover, upon its outer parts, the scroll-saw had done its worth." Yet Mr. Sells could visualize what might be done and over seven years the house was slowly changed and made both comfortable and attractive, a farm developed which supplied the family's rye flour and corn meal, as well as hams, bacon, fowls of every sort, and fruits and vegetables. Where lumber was needed, trees were cut down and milled in neighboring sawmills. He took especial pride in a yoke of oxen that were used for farm purposes. Springs were controlled and developed for water supply. A tennis court was made. A stable was built for the horses which Mr. Sells loved to ride and which gave him much of his exercise.

This "North Castle" farm was a haven for Mrs. Sells and the daughters, Marjorie and Dorothy. It was also a most profitable investment for Mr. Sells, physically and spiritually. In the deep peace of its winter evenings, he thought out straight things otherwise very puzzling. He could think out things of use to himself and also to his Firm and to the world at large. The problems of the farm diverted his thoughts from business and left him refreshed. He often stated that his best ideas in accountancy and organization came to him as he was "stumbling around" in the woods. He loved simplicity, he communed with nature.

Mr. Sells sold "North Castle" and acquired another estate near Greenwich, Connecticut. Here again he found the opportunity to refresh himself with things natural, with things simple. He added a hundred acres or more to this place in order to acquire a beautiful hemlock grove. He wanted to "stumble around."

Tennis had a great attraction for Mr. Sells and he continued this very active sport until within a year of the time of his death. It is given to few thus to maintain physical agility in the sixties. He was fond of playing with his daughter Marjorie. In later years, he often obtained his opponent's defeat by the use of strategy by which he more than made good his declining physical powers. In years gone by he had often played with Arthur Ruhl and Richard Harding Davis, the newspaper correspondents, and with other friends who lived in his immediate neighborhood.

Mr. Sells was much beloved by his neighbors—not less by the local farmers and laborers than by those who, like himself, owned estates as an incident to professional or business life in New York. He was more likely to acquire a plot of adjoining real estate in order to help a necessitous neighbor than he was to acquire it by reason of his own needs. He found much quiet amusement in things that would have annoyed the ordinary man. He was fond of telling how he bought a couple of barrels from a workman in his neighborhood. He paid for the barrels, and they were later delivered. A few weeks later the neighbor referred to the barrels that had been delivered and told Mr. Sells that he had probably forgotten about the matter of payment. Mr. Sells feigned forgetfulness and cheerfully paid for the barrels a second time. A few weeks later another neighbor, a friend of the first one, stopped Mr. Sells on the street and asked him if he had remembered receiving a couple of barrels a few weeks previously from him. He said he disliked to speak of the matter, but he imagined that Mr. Sells had forgotten to pay for the barrels. Mr. Sells expressed surprise and paid for the barrels a third time. The kindness and humor of this astute auditor, who had a remarkable memory for detailed transactions, and who had brought many a defaulter to book are apparent from this incident. He loved his fellow men and even found it possible to derive amusement from their simple attempts to deceive him.

Baker University bestowed upon Mr. Sells in 1909 the honorary degree of Master of Arts and New York University seven years later awarded him the honorary degree of Doctor of Commercial Science.

By his fellow-workers Mr. Sells was held in the highest professional regard, notably for his resourcefulness and skill in devising new methods to keep pace with the increasing complexities of industrial processes and business organization. For 21 years before his death in 1924 he was the senior administrator of the large and widely scattered organization which his Firm rapidly became. In the discharge of this responsibility, with its sometimes delicate problems of human sensibilities, he revealed exceptional qualities of mind and heart which brought him in full measure the respect and affection of his associates.

What may be regarded as the background of the firm of Haskins & Sells was the association of Mr. Haskins and Mr. Sells as professional accountants under an engagement from the Joint Commission of the Fifty-third Congress.

This Commission was appointed under an act of March 3, 1893, to "Inquire into and examine the status of the laws organizing the Executive Departments, Bureaus, Divisions and other government establishments at the National Capital; the rules, regulations, and methods for the conduct of the same; the time and attention devoted to the operations thereof by the persons employed therein and the grade of efficiency of all such employes; whether any modification of these laws can be made to secure greater efficiency and economy, and whether a reduction in the number or compensation of the persons authorized to be employes in the State Executive Departments or Bureaus can be made without injury to the public service."

The Commission was composed of Alex M. Dockery, Chairman, James D. Richardson and Nelson Dingley, Jr., members on the part of the House of Representatives, F. M. Cockrell, James K. Jones, and S. M. Cullen, members on the part of the Senate. The Commission was generally known as the "Dockery Commission." Mr. Dockery (of Missouri) had undertaken a pioneering task. At the time it was organized the general expectation of what the Commission might accomplish had been anything but optimistic, and in the lobbies of the Capitol the project was referred to as "Dockery's toy."

A few weeks later, however, the financial panic of May 1893 swept the nation into a severe depression, and the economy project began to be taken seriously. For the first time since the Civil War era the United States Treasury was showing an operating deficit. That in itself was a startling event and though the annual amount of the deficiency (reaching $70,000,000 in 1894) was microscopic by today's standards, it caused concern as being the equivalent of a quarter of a drastically shrunken total revenue. Press and public began to follow the work of the Commission and its experts with interest. The new President, Grover Cleveland, and the Congress showed an awareness of the need for modernizing antiquated methods, some of them dating from the era of Alexander Hamilton, and for cleaning house generally.

Under the act authorizing the Commission, provision was made

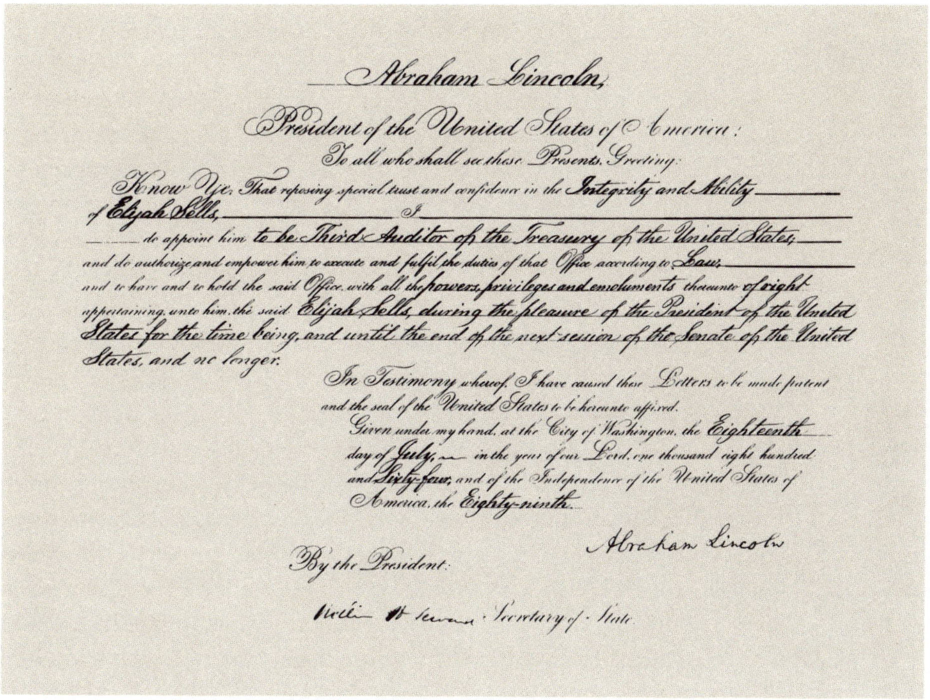

Abraham Lincoln,

President of the United States of America:

To all who shall see these Presents, Greeting:

Know Ye; That reposing special trust and confidence in the Integrity and Ability of Elijah Sells, I do appoint him to be Third Auditor of the Treasury of the United States; and do authorize and empower him to execute and fulfil the duties of that Office according to Law; and to have and to hold the said Office, with all the powers, privileges and emoluments thereunto of right appertaining, unto him, the said Elijah Sells, during the pleasure of the President of the United States for the time being, and until the end of the next session of the Senate of the United States, and no longer.

In Testimony whereof, I have caused these Letters to be made patent and the seal of the United States to be hereunto affixed.

Given under my hand, at the City of Washington, the Eighteenth day of July, in the year of our Lord, one thousand eight hundred and Sixty-four, and of the Independence of the United States of America, the Eighty-ninth.

Abraham Lincoln

By the President:

William H Seward Secretary of State.

"Know Ye; That reposing special trust and confidence in the Integrity and Ability of Elijah Sells . . ." wrote Abraham Lincoln in appointing the father of our founding partner Third Auditor of the Treasury of the United States on July 18, 1864,

for the employment of not to exceed three experts to render such assistance as the Commission might require.

Acting on Dockery's recommendation the Commission recruited as its chief expert Joseph W. Reinhart, President and formerly head of the Accounting Department of the Atchison, Topeka & Santa Fe Railroad. As an expert, Reinhart had brought about its reorganization, and had instituted accounting methods, which led to substantial cost reductions and greatly increased profits. His principal contribution to the Commission's work, however, was his appointment of two experts, whom he knew personally, as well as by reputation, Charles Waldo Haskins and Elijah Watts Sells. They met in Washington in June, 1893, and took up the work for the Commission.

The Commission's two full-time investigators had previously had extensive experience in financial and accounting pursuits. In their Washington survey they followed a plan of rendering interim reports, and as they progressed from one department to another they submitted a series of recommendations on a wide range of accounting and administrative matters. These were received with a surprisingly large measure of approval by the responsible administrative officials and many of them were put promptly into effect by Executive Order or legislative action. When the Commission was automatically dissolved by the expiration of the 53rd Congress on March 4, 1895, new systems of accounting and auditing had been installed in the various departments, economies aggregating $600,000 a year had been definitely effected and recommendations involving further annual savings of $400,000 made. The competence and skill of the two associates had been praised in the highest terms on the floor of the Senate by Hon. Redfield Proctor of Vermont, and they had received the thanks of the Chairman of the Congressional Commission in a formal communication, of which the following is an extract:

> "To your rare business capacity and peculiar adaptation to analyzing old and formulating plans for new Methods, is in great measure due the credit for the reorganization of the accounting system of the United States Government. It was in many respects the most extensive and important undertaking of the kind in the history of the Country, and its success in expediting and simplifying the public business without removing any of the necessary safeguards has been fully demonstrated and attested by all of the officials affected thereby."

2

The Formation of the Firm of Haskins & Sells—
City of Chicago Engagement—Early Offices—
Early Engagements—Charles S. Ludlam—Homer A. Dunn

The close and cordial association of the two men in this work for the Dockery Commission, and the feeling of mutual respect which came out of it foreshadowed the establishment of a continuing professional relationship; and they felt some confidence that, despite hard times, business would come to their doors. So it was that from their new quarters in an office building at 2 Nassau Street in New York the two partners on March 4, 1895 made a public offer of their services.

The partnership was actually a continuation of the practice of public accounting which Mr. Haskins had commenced in 1886, and the first clients were those that Mr. Haskins had served from 1886 to 1895.

The partnership agreement was simple, showing the confidence they had in each other.

> *Agreement*
>
> Entered into this fourth day of March, eighteen hundred and ninety-five, by and between *C. W. Haskins* and *E. W. Sells*, parties hereto:
>
> To associate themselves in the business and profession of making examinations of accounts and records, reports and certificates, and investigations of the affairs of institutions, and to plan and inaugurate accounting systems for corporations, trustees, assignees, receivers, committees, courts, municipalities and governments, either temporarily or permanently.
>
> To have an office in the City of New York. The expense for assistance of others that may be employed, rent, and other items incident to an office, shall be the only expenses incurred, and it

shall be by the consent of both parties hereto and borne equally by them.

To charge for the services to be performed under this agreement not less than twenty-five dollars per day for each while employed and necessary traveling and subsistence expenses when engaged away from New York City, when for temporary service. Fixed rates per month or per annum for regular engagements may be made by the consent of both parties hereto.

It shall be the purpose of the parties hereto to utilize the services of both as far as possible in every instance, so that the work performed may be joint; but when the services of but one of the parties can be utilized, all reports, certificates and statements prepared must have the assent of the other party when practicable before they are rendered.

The collections for services performed by both parties shall be divided equally with the other and such division shall be made on the first of every month or oftener.

This association may be dissolved on thirty days notice in writing by either party to the other, provided that any temporary work that may be in hand shall be completed in accordance with the terms hereof.

Signed in duplicate. C. W. Haskins

E. W. Sells

In the first announcement which the Firm sent out, and which, it should be mentioned, was before the days of state recognition of accountancy, or societies of certified public accountants or committees on professional ethics, attention was invited to the qualifications of the firm members, the kinds of clients who might need their services, and the nature of the services they offered to render.

Among the Firm's first engagements, in April 1895, was an examination of the methods of accounting at Vassar College. It came through Mr. S. D. Coykendall, one of the trustees of Vassar College. Mr. Coykendall, or his son, was a client of the Firm for a long time thereafter. Another of the Coykendall engagements was one of the earliest American corporations, the Rhinebeck and Kingston Ferry Company organized in 1783.

The engagements which followed embraced services for the Government, states, municipalities, insurance companies, banks and

C. W. HASKINS,
E. W. SELLS,
NO. 2 NASSAU STREET.

NEW YORK, March 4, 1895.

Having concluded our special engagement with the United States Government as Experts for the Joint Commission of the Fifty-third Congress, authorized by law to examine the Executive Departments,

WE OFFER OUR SERVICES TO

CORPORATIONS, TRUSTEES, ASSIGNEES, RECEIVERS, COMMITTEES,
COURTS, MUNICIPALITIES, ETC.,

TO MAKE

PERIODICAL AND SPECIAL EXAMINATIONS OF ACCOUNTS AND RECORDS,
INVESTIGATIONS OF AFFAIRS,
REPORTS AND CERTIFICATES,

AND

TO INTRODUCE

SIMPLE AND EFFICIENT METHODS OF ACCOUNTING.

Our experience has covered a period of over twenty years in the operating, accounting, and financial departments of railroads and other corporations having large and diversified interests, and we have accomplished a complete revision of the accounting system of the United States Government.

C. W. HASKINS.
E. W. SELLS.

HON. REDFIELD PROCTOR, of Vermont, said in the United States Senate, on July 15, 1894:

"In regard to the experts who were employed by the Commission, I have seen much of them, and spent a good deal of time with them in going over the details of their recommendations. I have the very highest opinion of their ability. I think the Commission was peculiarly fortunate in their selection. I confess my only surprise was that they were so very fortunate. These experts are men thoroughly competent, experienced, and skilful, and have been extremely careful and conservative in their methods. . . ."

OFFICE OF THE JOINT COMMISSION OF CONGRESS TO INQUIRE INTO THE STATUS OF LAWS
ORGANIZING THE EXECUTIVE DEPARTMENTS.

WASHINGTON, D. C., March 2, 1895.

MESSRS. C. W. HASKINS and E. W. SELLS, Experts under the Joint Commission, etc.

GENTLEMEN:—In concluding the work of this Commission, it affords me especial pleasure to express to you appreciation of the valuable services you have rendered.

To your rare business capacity, and peculiar adaptation to analyzing old and formulating plans for new methods, in great measure is due the credit for the reorganization of the accounting system of the United States Government. It was in many respects the most extensive and important undertaking of the kind in the history of the country, and its success in expediting and simplifying the public business without removing any of the necessary safeguards has been fully demonstrated and attested by all of the officials affected thereby.

Very respectfully,
(Signed) ALEX. M. DOCKERY,
Chairman, Joint Commission.

The first public announcement of Haskins & Sells is typical of the manner in which professional offices offered their services before the turn of the century.

industrial companies, street and steam railways, mercantile and industrial organizations of every description. The services of the Firm on account of the extensive railroad experience of the founders were in large demand for railroad work. During the period of these engagements, the Firm received considerable publicity through the discovery of many serious irregularities in the accounts of the auditor of one of the railroads in the South and his conviction on their testimony furnished at the trial.

The offices were removed on May 1, 1896 to the Johnston Building, 30 Broad Street, in which building Haskins & Sells were the first tenants. A photograph taken in the office in 1899 shows mature accountants with mustaches and beards, stiff wing collars, and ascot ties.

The growing practice in the Middle West led to the opening of an office in the Marquette Building, 204 Dearborn Street, Chicago, on December 1, 1900. The importance of this step was apparent when the City of Chicago engagement soon followed.

On June 24, 1901, the City Council of Chicago passed an order authorizing the Mayor, Comptroller, and Chairman of the Committee on Finance to engage a firm of accountants to introduce and supervise a uniform system of the City Government.

In compliance with this order, the Committee entered into an agreement with Haskins & Sells, Certified Public Accountants, under which they made, during the year 1901, a study of the laws of the State of Illinois and the ordinances of the City of Chicago, and of the accounting methods then in vogue, and the methods required under a modern and comprehensive system of accounting for the conduct of the finances and affairs of the City of Chicago throughout all of its various branches, divisions, bureaus, and offices.

It was the desire of the City administration that the accounting system of the City of Chicago, covering all of its fiscal transactions, should be made as clear and efficient as the accounting systems in use by the most advanced of the great industrial, manufacturing, and transportation companies. The accountants were requested to proceed on these lines without any restrictions other than those imposed by the laws and they were given the earnest support of the administration in all of their efforts.

On November 20, 1901, Haskins & Sells submitted a report outlining a system of municipal accounts for the City of Chicago, accompanied by schedules, defining the operations of the system in each of the

The Haskins & Sells professional and office staff looked its best for its 1899 portrait. Wide lapels and abundant beards and moustaches show indebtedness of today's "new" styles to the past.

various departments, bureaus, and offices of the City Government, and also, by forms of the necessary books, blanks, and reports. This report included a revision of all the ordinances required thereby.

On December 23, 1901, the City Council passed an ordinance making "the system of accounting and auditing prepared by Haskins & Sells, Certified Public Accountants, as shown in their report, with the accompanying exhibits, submitted to the said Council under date of November 20, 1901, the official accounting and auditing system of the City of Chicago."

The contract made with Haskins & Sells provided that they should "supervise the introduction and inauguration of said system of accounting, accounting methods and auditing the opening of the books and records of account and audit necessitated and provided for thereby, and the preparation of all portions of the Annual Reports relating to the receipt accounting for and disbursement of moneys, for the year 1902."

The new system of accounting was inaugurated January 1, 1902 and achieved great success. It not only effected economies during the first year of operation amounting to $72,630, but resulted in an increase of $425,000 in miscellaneous revenues. The City Controller in his first report issued under the new system said:

> "The change from the old to the new method was accomplished without confusion or detriment to the conduct of public affairs, and the detail workings of the new system have since progressed without friction. It is now evident that the system has proved an advantage to the City Government; that it has improved the efficiency of individual employes and prompted an intelligent and interested direction of their efforts by department heads."

The year nineteen hundred and one saw the first evidence of international expansion. Under date of April 10, 1901, the Firm announced the opening of an office in London. This followed an engagement for an American client—the Barnum and Bailey Circus—which had accounting and financial problems arising out of taking the Circus to England. Mr. Haskins and Mr. Sells were aware of other American organizations planning activities in Europe and it seemed to them that a base in London would be desirable. The Firm's first merger took place there as the firm of Conant & Grant with offices at 30 Coleman Street in the "City" was acquired. Grant came to the United States and Conant managed the London Office. The practice in London was not large and it was ten years before any profit was shown, but it did serve the purpose of a base for European engagements. As the practice increased, the London Office moved to Bush House and then to Queens House on Kingsway. This was fortunate as the German Blitz of September 1941 leveled the Coleman Street area.

In the United States the Firm served an important and varied group of clients. Some of the engagements of the Firm in 1902 were:

Philadelphia & Reading Railroad Co.
United States Rubber Company
Erie Railroad Co.
Vassar College
Cincinnati & New Orleans Railroad
American Trust Co.—Cleveland
Wheeling & Lake Erie Railroad
St. Louis Street Railways
John Muir & Co.
New York University
American Express Co.—London and Paris
Borden's Condensed Milk Co.
City of New Rochelle
Presbyterian Hospital
Atlantic Coast Line Railroad Co.
Atlanta and West Point Railroad Co.
The Western Railway of Alabama

Some of these remain as clients: United States Rubber Company (now Uniroyal, Inc.), Erie Railroad Co. (now Erie-Lackawanna), New York University, Presbyterian Hospital, Atlantic Coast Line Railroad Co., Atlanta and West Point Railroad Co., and The Western Railway of Alabama.

A considerable demand for the Firm's services in and about St. Louis, especially in connection with the street railways, led to the opening of an office there on January 20, 1902.

During the same year, or specifically June 2, 1902, an office was opened in Cleveland. Pittsburgh followed July 1, 1903.

Two of the experienced railroad accountants who were brought into the organization at an early date were Charles Stewart Ludlam and Homer Adams Dunn.

Charles S. Ludlam became associated with the Firm in 1895

Charles Stewart Ludlam, managing partner from 1924 to 1930, was an acute analyst of business affairs who believed that esteem for the profession would result from doing good work.

and became a partner in 1903. He was the third of three who guided the destinies of the organization in its period of early growth and was from 1924 to 1930 the active head of the Firm.

Mr. Ludlam was born in Chicago, November 11, 1866. At the age of 14 he entered the employ of Pullman Company as an office boy, advancing to bookkeeper of the company's capital stock accounts. Moving to Albuquerque for his health, he was there employed for several years in the accounting department of Atlantic & Pacific Railroad Company and later became general bookkeeper of The Colorado Midland Railway Company. For several years therafter he was employed by J. J. Hagerman, a Colorado capitalist, as general accountant and auditor of various railroad, construction, mining, irrigation, and land companies. He left this work to join Haskins & Sells.

Mr. Ludlam represented the Firm on numerous accounting, auditing, and system engagements of importance in themselves and in enhancing the professional reputation of the Firm. Notable among them was the complex task of overhauling the accounting and auditing systems of the City of Chicago. He was also in charge of the accounting work incident to a reorganization of the street railways of St. Louis, and the accounting aspects of rate cases affecting Oklahoma, Missouri and Arkansas railroads. On the latter the Kansas City Star reported June 17, 1913:

> "Millions of figures were the contribution of A. P. Taliaferro and C. S. Ludlam, names now practically forgotten in Missouri, to Missouri's great victory in the railroad rate cases yesterday. They represented the firm of accountants selected by the state, Haskins & Sells.
>
> When Herbert S. Hadley, then attorney general, commenced the suits to enforce the freight and passenger rate laws, he employed Haskins & Sells. That firm's representatives burrowed into the railroads' books, analyzed their earnings, how the new laws would affect the railroads and presented their findings in charts. On the witness stand the attorneys for the railroads could not budge them an inch from their findings and even the court complimented them on their work.
>
> 'Those two men deserve more credit for Missouri's victory in the rate cases than all the lawyers together in the cases,' Sanford B. Ladd, one of the state's attorneys, said. 'The lawyers worked days and slept nights. These two men worked day and

> night and presented such an array of figures and such careful analyses of the railroads' earnings that ultimate victory came to the state.' "

After the First World War Mr. Ludlam was chief accountant for the United States Liquidation Commission, which handled extensive settlements between the United States and the European Allies.

He was a Certified Public Accountant of New York, Pennsylvania, Ohio, Illinois, Missouri, and Oklahoma, becoming a member of several accounting societies and of the Board of Examiners and the Council of the American Institute of Accountants. He was author of "Treatment of Sinking Funds" and "Methods of Accounting and Auditing in a Bond House."

Mr. Ludlam was an acute analyst of business affairs. He was extraordinarily gifted in the interpretation of accounts in a clear and practical manner which commanded the respect of business executives. An indefatigable worker himself, working on occasion 24 and even 36 hours at a stretch, he always received the hearty support of his co-workers, and acquired a reputation which reached beyond his own organization, for willingness and ability to execute any engagement, whatever might be the difficulties of shortages of staff or urgencies of deadlines. In his belief, which he often expressed, the chief influence in the growth of the profession in public esteem would lie in doing good work; and he lived up fully to the implications of his convictions.

As a personal note, Mr. Ludlam was ambidextrous in golf and could also write captions with his left hand and fill in the figures with his right.

He was forceful and incisive in action with great drive and withal most considerate of the men who worked under him. He demanded complete honesty, integrity, and loyalty. His world was Haskins & Sells, without outside interests except for golf, and any indication of disloyalty or failure to put Haskins & Sells first distressed him. As further evidence of his dedication to the Firm, on his death his entire estate went eventually to the Haskins & Sells Foundation.

On the death of Mr. Sells in 1924, Mr. Ludlam became the Managing Partner of the Firm, continuing until his retirement in 1930. He went to live in Florida where he died in 1934.

Homer Adams Dunn, who came into Haskins & Sells in 1902, spent his youth under conditions which developed in him a fine

Homer Adams Dunn, an original thinker who was a leader in developing the early technical procedures of the Firm.

character and capacity for hard work. His father, Stephen Hendershot Dunn, was born in New York State and his mother in Maine. They were married in Piqua, Ohio and lived there for a time near the then western frontier, migrating to Kansas, where Homer was born on April 22, 1863 in the family homestead at Valley Falls, Kansas, a very small town on the Atchison, Topeka & Santa Fe Railroad, twenty-five miles northeast of Topeka and in a more or less unsettled country, invaded at times by Indians. He started his business career at the age of 16 as Deputy Postmaster at Valley Falls, moving the next year to become a night telegraph operator at Valley Falls for the Atchison, Topeka & Santa Fe Railroad. For one school year in 1880-81 he attended Washburn College in Topeka, but returned in March 1881 to his post as night operator at Valley Falls.

In August 1881 he was transferred to Augusta, Kansas, first as acting agent and then relief agent, operator, and dispatcher. Ambitious to get ahead, in December 1881 (now 18) he secured a transfer to the Shops Office of the Railroad in Topeka to permit the completion of the study of stenography. He became stenographer and clerk with the Missouri & Kansas Telephone Company and the United Telegraph Company in August 1882. (Incidentally, he never forgot his stenography and used it in later life to make rapid notes.) His restless ambition brought him back a year later to the Atchison, Topeka & Santa Fe in Topeka as a stenographer and clerk to the General Freight Agent, and in 1884 to Kansas City, Fort Scott & Memphis Railroad as stenographer and clerk to the Comptroller, and in 1888 to Memphis as Freight and Passenger Accountant for the Kansas City, Memphis & Birmingham Railroad. He briefly held a position in a law office, where he read Blackstone and other standard works, but decided not to follow law.

Elijah Watt Sells had served the Atchison, Topeka & Santa Fe Railroad and some of its subsidiaries, and he became Secretary and Auditor of The Colorado Midland Railway Company at Colorado Springs. He drew Homer Dunn into his office as Chief Clerk in December 1888, where Dunn remained until Mr. Sells went to Chicago in 1893 in connection with the consolidation of offices. In this same consolidation Homer Dunn was transferred to Topeka, Kansas as Chief Clerk of the Collateral Property Accounts, a group of eight coal companies, ten land and town companies, two water companies, three mercantile companies, a grain elevator company, and a hospital association.

With the death of the Auditor of the Atchison, Topeka & Santa Fe Railroad Company in August 1896 Homer Dunn was given charge of the General Auditor's office as Chief Clerk. With further consolidation of offices he was appointed on December 1, 1896 as Assistant Auditor of Disbursements in Topeka.

With the founding of the firm of Haskins & Sells in 1895 engagements were secured from various railroads including the Central of Georgia Railway Company at Savannah, Georgia of which Mr. Haskins had been Comptroller. The need of a strong and competent auditor became evident and on December 24, 1896 Mr. Sells wrote to Homer Dunn asking if he would be interested, if openings came in the east "for first class railroad accountants, like yourself."

Mr. Dunn replied promptly that there was nothing to hold him in Topeka, if a suitable opportunity arose. On January 18, 1897 Mr. Sells said the opening was for the Auditorship of the Central of Georgia Railway in Savannah, where there was need for the entire revision of its accounting methods. While there was some discussion as to whether the salary would be $275 or $300 a month, Mr. Dunn accepted the post as of February 1, 1897. He did revise the accounting system and devised the first successful system of billing freight through from initial steamship ports to interior railway destinations.

He remained with the Central of Georgia Railway until June 1902, when Mr. Sells persuaded him to go with Haskins & Sells in New York.

Homer Dunn was a person of great tenacity of purpose and an indomitable will to do thorough work, having no patience with inefficiency. With his varied and responsible accounting background in railroads and his strong personality he soon became one of the most important men in the firm of Haskins & Sells.

During the First World War, Mr. Dunn was head of the Bureau of Audits of the Alien Property Custodian's office.

He was active in professional matters, serving as Secretary of the New York State Board of C.P.A. Examiners, President of the National Association of C.P.A. Examiners, Chairman of the New York State C.P.A. Committee on Grievances, and President of the American Society of Certified Public Accountants.

Among his writings were papers on "Accounting Inconsistencies and Fallacies," "Information Needs of Investors for Judgment of Public Utilities," "Railway Accounting in Its Relation to the Twentieth Section of the Act to Regulate Commerce," "Uniform Accounting

Methods for Anthracite Coal Operations."

Mr. Dunn was one of the best grounded practitioners of public accountancy of his time. Widely versed in accounting and auditing methods and an original thinker, he was a leader in developing the early technical procedures of the Firm. He was a close student of business affairs and took a constructive part in the development of commercial arbitration, becoming a director of the American Arbitration Association. In his long career of intense and seemingly tireless activity there were always apparent the workings of a fertile and forceful mind which commanded the strong respect of his fellow workers. This forcefulness made him a difficult person at times for he never hesitated to state his mind to his partners, in caustic letters to the newspapers, and in strong and often controversial positions in professional societies. As a result of his restless youth in rustic surroundings, his speech was interlarded with forceful and often profane interjections, strangely so natural as to be inoffensive. While his positive convictions were stated in a super-positive manner, there was always a feeling on the part of those listening that there was great sincerity and wide experience back of his remarks. His rugged exterior concealed a kindly heart.

Also as a result of his youth, he was an "out-of-doors" man, an enthusiastic horseman, and a persistent, if not a great golfer.

On his death in 1935, one of the leaders of the accounting profession, Charles S. McCulloch, wrote feelingly of him, concluding the eulogy: "He loved his profession and was tireless in his efforts in its behalf. In his latter years, after retiring from active practice, he devoted practically his entire time and thought to the advancement of accountancy."

3

Haskins & Sells at the end of 1902—
The death of Charles Waldo Haskins—The Formation of the Corporation of "Haskins & Sells Certified Public Accountants"—
The Resumption of the Partnership

At the end of 1902 there were two partners, C. W. Haskins and E. W. Sells, four managers: H. W. Brown, New York; T. B. Dixey, New York; L. O. Fisher, Cleveland; F. K. Parke, Chicago and five principals: L. H. Conant, New York; H. A. Dunn, New York; D. S. Fero, New York; James Grant, New York; C. S. Ludlam, New York; seventy-eight accountants, including eight who later became partners (W. P. Bickett, C. E. Morris, D. C. Morris, C. E. Scoville, L. N. Simson, A. S. Vaughan, Finley Wharton, and P. G. White), ten assistant accountants, and office staff of twenty-eight (including H. B. Cook, stenographer, who became a partner, and Sarah I. Bolles, who was later and for many years Firm Secretary).

At that moment a heavy blow came in the sudden death of Mr. Haskins on January 9, 1903. The loss shook Mr. Sells personally for he and Mr. Haskins had spent ten years in very close personal association. It was also a great blow to the young Firm for Mr. Haskins was a great and dynamic leader widely known in the industrial and financial world. In addition, Mr. Haskins had supplied the major part of the Capital of the Firm. Mr. Haskins and Mr. Sells each had Capital of $75,000.00, and Mr. Haskins had advanced an additional $60,000.00.

"The Firm had a rapid growth in the first seven years of its history, increasing its gross revenue from $14,856. in the fiscal year ended May 31, 1896 to $340,315. in the fiscal year ended May 31, 1902. The engagements were varied—public utilities, municipalities and even corporate consolidations including William Ziegler's consolidation of baking powder companies and the consolidation of fifty companies into the American Glass Company."

The balance sheet of the Firm at the death of Mr. Haskins (the close of business January 8, 1903) was:

Assets		
Cash and Cash Items		$ 36,901.12
Accounts Receivable		
Current	$166,122.11	
Unfinished Engagements	95,530.51	261,652.62
Interest Accrued		1,633.68
Furniture and Fixtures		5,014.04
Total		$305,201.46
Liabilities		
Loans—C. W. Haskins, Trustee		$ 60,000.00
Payroll		5,855.70
Accounts Payable		2,144.12
Interest Payable		2,438.66
Country Club Land Association		540.00
American Surety Company Surety Bond		1,000.00
Estate of C. W. Haskins		32,000.30
E. W. Sells		8,767.57
C. S. Ludlam		13,142.00
D. S. Fero		3,740.19
L. H. Conant		10,207.59
James Grant		1,849.58
H. A. Dunn		3,146.13
Expenses Accrued		369.62
Reserve—City of Chicago		10,000.00
Capital		
Estate of C. W. Haskins	$75,000.00	
E. W. Sells	75,000.00	150,000.00
Total		$305,201.46

Mr. Sells' thirty years of business experience, his administrative capacity, his keenness in discerning talent, and his ability to understand human relations and tie people to him, all combined to enable him to close the ranks and continue the Firm's growth and development.

To continue the name of Haskins & Sells, to find a way to hold the fine group of men who had been gathered into the organization and to finance the payment of Mr. Haskins' Capital and loans, the idea occurred to Mr. Sells of incorporating the Firm and offering stock in it to the important men on the staff. It was a bold and unusual plan. Mr.

Sells consulted Charles S. Atterbury of the firm of Atterbury & Mullally, who examined the laws of both New Jersey and New York and found no bar to the incorporation. There was no problem in using the simple name Haskins & Sells, but Mr. Sells wished to add "Certified Public Accountants." With Mr. Atterbury's advice Mr. Sells secured the approval of the Secretary of the Board of Regents, Mr. Parsons, and also the Attorney General, John C. Cuneen.

The corporation of "Haskins & Sells, Certified Public Accountants" was organized January 26, 1903 with the following incorporators: Elijah W. Sells, Leonard H. Conant, Charles S. Ludlam, DeRoy S. Fero and Leon O. Fisher. The stated purposes were:

"To examine accounts, finances, debts, assets and property, to make audits and appraisals, to design and introduce systems of accounting, and generally to do all things within the scope of professional accountants, of, for and in connection with corporations, firms, individuals, states, governments, municipalities, and all other institutions and concerns, and to make reports upon and in connection with the same with such expert investigation and examination as may be desired, including therein the employment of all engineering, mechanical and other experts as may be necessary or convenient.

To take over, assume and carry on the accounting business of the late firm of Haskins & Sells, Certified Public Accountants in the City of New York, including the acquisition of all their assets, property, business and goodwill.

To engage generally in the business of Public Accountants, and as such to incur indebtedness and acquire such property, real and personal, as may be found necessary or convenient in the prosecution thereof."

The capital stock was $600,000.00 of which $300,000.00 was preferred and $300,000.00 common.

The control and management was to be vested in the hands of the holders of the common stock provided dividends were paid on the preferred.

The first officers were:

E. W. Sells	President
C. S. Ludlam	Vice President
D. S. Fero	Vice President
H. A. Dunn	Vice President
L. H. Conant	Vice President and Treasurer
H. B. Cook	Secretary

In addition there were as directors L. O. Fisher and Morris W. Mundy (representing Mrs. Haskins).

Of the preferred stock $75,000.00 was allotted to Mrs. Henrietta S. Haskins and $75,000.00 to Elijah Watt Sells. The balance was paid for in cash by Mr. Sells and fifteen of the important men in the organization, each receiving one share of common stock for each share of the preferred purchased.

The Corporation continued the practice of the former Firm. However, early in 1906 there was a good deal of agitation from other accountants and some inquiries from clients as to the character of the organization. It was, therefore, decided to change the form and once again to have the practice conducted by a partnership. Accordingly by an agreement dated January 2, 1907 between "Haskins & Sells, Certified Public Accountants" (a corporation) and Elijah W. Sells, Charles S. Ludlam, DeRoy S. Fero and Homer A. Dunn, co-partners, who on December 20, 1906 joined themselves in a co-partnership for the purpose of engaging in the practice of Public Accounting under the firm name of Haskins & Sells, the Corporation transferred to the co-partnership the full right and title to the use of its properties, professional goodwill, and the name of Haskins & Sells. The Corporation then (on March 30, 1907) changed its name to Haskins & Sells Company. The capital stock was later reduced to $500.00. In 1920 the Certificate of Incorporation was amended to include the right to acquire real property, and through it an office building was acquired in 1920 at 37 West 39th Street. The building was leased to Haskins & Sells. It was sold in 1925. The Corporation has continued to be in existence as it protects the name of Haskins & Sells in New York. The stock, nominally in the names of five partners of Haskins & Sells, and with nominal assets of $500.00, is beneficially owned by Haskins & Sells.

4

The Insurance Engagements of 1905—
Other Important Engagements 1903-1909—
Haskins & Sells Athletic Association—Howard B. Cook—
Charles E. Morris—Arthur S. Vaughan—John F. Forbes

In the Spring of nineteen hundred and five there was much concern in New York over the administration of the three leading insurance companies. Investigations were made not only by the State Insurance Department, but by insurance companies themselves. Public Accountants were in each instance retained to examine into the financial affairs and report. Two firms of accountants were selected in each case to collaborate. Haskins & Sells were engaged in all three of the cases, working in conjunction with Deloitte, Plender, Griffiths & Co., one of the leading firms of English Chartered Accountants, on two of the companies and with Price Waterhouse & Co. on the Equitable Life Assurance Society. Two of the engagements involved lengthy investigations and voluminous reports resulting in rather complete reorganization of the respective accounting systems. In the third case the conditions revealed less necessity for a thorough investigation. These engagements served probably to bring the Firm into public eye more than anything in its history. Out of this work arose the Firm's engagement for the Equitable Life Assurance Society of the United States, which has continued to be a client.

The steady growth of the Firm from 1903 to 1909 is evident in the list of engagements for clients still served:

1903 Central of Georgia Railway Co.
International Harvester Co.
1904 Louisville & Nashville Railroad Co.
The A. S. Abell Company
1905 Community Service Society of New York

Catholic University of America
Dow Chemical Company
Equitable Life Assurance Society of the United States
1906 Mercantile Safe Deposit & Trust Company of Baltimore
J. H. Oliphant & Co.
Lehigh University
1908 Goulds Pumps Incorporated
1909 Life Insurance Association of America
American Manufacturing Co.

The accountants in the first decade of the twentieth century worked hard and often long hours. However, there were diversions. Mr. Sells was interested in sports and enjoyed horseback riding. He also organized the Haskins & Sells Athletic Association, the activities of which centered around baseball and tennis. The baseball team included many whose names were prominent in Haskins & Sells history—among them six who later became partners: Thomas N. Willins, Howard B. Cook, John R. Wildman, Edward Fuller, Charles S. Ludlam, and DeRoy S. Fero. Mr. Sells developed a baseball team on his farm at North Castle and competed with the Firm team. The latter was usually the winner, until partly in jest Mr. Sells hired some of the professionals from the New York Giants and dressed them in farm clothes—with the natural result of humbling the Haskins & Sells team.

The baseball games ended in picnic suppers prepared and served by the women in the office.

In tennis, Arthur M. Lovibond, ranking among the first ten in the Country, coached the players.

Considerable time elapsed after the opening of the office in Pittsburgh before another office was added to the list. During the Fall of nineteen hundred and ten, however, the need for representation in the vicinity of Baltimore became sufficient to warrant opening an office there. This was done on December 1, 1910 with Edward Fuller as Manager. Mr. Fuller became a partner in 1913.

The year 1910 also saw the elevation to partnership of four men who had been part of the early organization: Howard B. Cook, Charles E. Morris, Arthur S. Vaughan, and Dudley C. Morris. Mr. Cook came from Atlanta, where after graduating from High School he became a stenographer with the Atlanta and West Point Railroad Co. and The Western Railway of Alabama, which were clients of Haskins & Sells

The Haskins & Sells baseball team of 1907. To humble them, their opponents were reinforced by "ringers" from the New York Giants.

handled by Mr. Sells. In 1899 Mr. Sells brought Mr. Cook to New York as a stenographer. He entered the new School of Commerce, Accounts and Finance at New York University, when Mr. Haskins was still Dean, and graduated with the Class of 1903. He secured his New York State CPA Certificate in 1907, and joined the New York State Society of Certified Public Accountants in that year, becoming its President in 1923. In that year, desirous of enjoying a life in early retirement, he resigned from the Firm, purchased a chateau in France and moved there with his family. The boom in securities in the later twenties attracted him strongly and he became deeply involved in the market. Unfortunately for him, he was on a steamship bound for New York when the market broke in 1929 and he was wiped out. He tried an accounting association with George M. Dallas, who had resigned from the Firm in 1931, and then became manager of a New York brokerage house. Both of these were unsuccessful, and he returned to Haskins & Sells in 1935, retiring in 1945, and dying in 1954.

Charles E. Morris was born in Virginia in 1867. The family later moved to Athens, Georgia, when Mr. Morris' father was elected Professor of English at the University of Georgia. Mr. Morris graduated from that University in 1886. While there he was active in athletics, being one of the star pitchers on the College baseball team. He had eight years experience with railroads ending in 1896 with the position of chief clerk for the consolidated railroads of Kansas City, Memphis and Birmingham, and the Kansas City, Fort Scott and Memphis Railroad. He came to New York in 1899 and secured a position with Haskins & Sells in July 1900.

He was soon involved in important engagements in Chicago, where he secured an Illinois CPA Certificate under the waiver provisions. He later obtained Certificates in New York, Pennsylvania, and Florida. He was made Manager of the London Office in 1904. Evidence of his growth and importance was his attendance at a meeting of principals and managers in May 1907 at which there were also present: E. W. Sells, D. S. Fero, F. A. Cleveland, A. S. Vaughan, D. C. Morris, C. S. Ludlam, H. A. Dunn, Finley Wharton, and A. P. Taliaferro.

In August 1907 he was assigned as a principal in New York with continuing charge and direction of the London Office. He spent considerable time out of the Country on work—England and Spain in 1907, and Japan, Philippine Islands, New Zealand, and Netherlands in 1909, and Cuba in 1913 and 1914. Much of this was for Westinghouse

Charles E. Morris, partner in charge of our first engagement for General Motors Corporation in 1919 and a widely traveled international accountant.

Electric & Mfg. Company in connection with which he also spent many months at the plants in Russia.

He was also in Russia in 1911 in connection with the acquisition of a plant by International Harvester Company. In a letter to New York from Paris in 1911 there was reference to 100,000 rubles of raw materials on the books which did not exist, and of large quantities of obsolete and worthless articles valued at full price. It was evidently a long and troublesome engagement with many complications due to Russian red tape.

Mr. Morris was in charge of the audit of Hyatt Roller Bearing Company of Harrison, New Jersey in 1914-1916 prior to the acquisition of Hyatt by United Motors whose assets were acquired by General Motors. Alfred P. Sloan, Jr. had been with Hyatt since 1895, and his father helped to finance it in 1898. Sloan became the dominant factor in it, and he became acquainted with Mr. Morris and developed a high regard for him. Consequently, when United Motors was formed he brought Mr. Morris and Haskins & Sells in as auditors, and then into General Motors Corporation when it was formed.

In Mr. Sloan's book "My Years With General Motors" he said:

> "I was of two minds about Mr. Durant. I admired his automotive genius, his imagination, his generous human qualities, and his integrity. His loyalty to the enterprise was absolute. I recognized, as Mr. Raskob and Pierre S. du Pont had, that he had created and inspired the dynamic growth of General Motors. But I thought he was too casual in his ways for an administrator, and he overloaded himself. Important decisions had to wait until he was free, and were often made impulsively. Two examples from my personal experience:
>
> My office was next door to his in the old General Motors Building on New York's Fifty-Seventh Street. I would sometimes go in to see him. One day in 1919 I went in and told him that I thought that, in view of the large public interest in the corporation's shares, we should have an independent audit by a certified public accountant. Our books were not being so audited, though they had been earlier under the bankers' regime. Mr. Durant did not have a sound concept of accounting as such and did not realize its great significance in administration. However, when I spoke to him about it, he said at once that he agreed with me and told me

> to go and get one. That was the way he worked. He had a financial department to handle affairs of that kind, but since I had made the suggestion I got the assignment. I brought in the firm of Haskins & Sells, which had audited the accounts of United Motors. This firm still audits General Motors acounts."*

Mr. Morris was an avid reader on a wide range of subjects on all of which he could converse with ease, an excellent golfer, a fine bridge player, and very skillful at billiards. His dedication to work was such that when on March 11, 1917 he married Ethel Bryant the only evidence in the office was that he wore a new string tie.

Arthur Stuart Vaughan was born in Richmond, Virginia June 1, 1869. About 1880 his family moved to Cincinnati, and he attended Woodward High School there graduating in 1888. He then obtained a position in the Comptroller's Office of the Cincinnati, New Orleans and Texas Pacific Railway Company. The President of this Company was Mr. John Scott, who in the late eighties had been President of The Colorado Midland Railway Company when Elijah Watt Sells was its Secretary and Auditor. Through Mr. Scott, Arthur Vaughan served in other railroad organizations.

In the winter of 1894-95, when Mr. Scott and Mr. Vaughan were alone in Mr. Scott's office at 46 Wall Street, New York, Mr. Haskins and Mr. Sells came in to see Mr. Scott. They said their work for the Government was about finished and they had decided to go into partnership and were planning to open an office in New York. They invited Mr. Scott to join them in the new undertaking, but after a long discussion he decided not to do so.

Between 1897 and 1900, while in Mr. Scott's employ, Mr. Vaughan conducted several examinations for Haskins & Sells, and in December 1900 entered the employ of Haskins & Sells.

He became a CPA in New York on July 30, 1901 (Certificate 187).

In October 1902 he was transferred to the Chicago Office of Haskins & Sells, which had been opened in 1900 and which had gone through the important and trying engagement for the City of Chicago. He became Manager of the Chicago Office May 1, 1903.

He was brought to New York in 1912 to take over the supervision of the Report Department, which also involved the supervision of all of the Firm's reports. In the course of this he made many trips to the offices to review reports in the field. He was most meticulous as to the content and wording of reports, always pressing for high standards of work and presentation. He later took over the supervision of the Financial Department. In those days he signed the entire semi-monthly payroll of every office of the Firm.

In 1912 John Franklin Forbes became a member of the Firm through the consolidation of his practice in San Francisco with that of the Firm. This connection arose in an interesting way. One of the sources of business for Haskins & Sells in its early days was a financier by the name of Patrick Calhoun. Among his many interests was the United Railways of San Francisco. Haskins & Sells made the audit of this Company in 1904 and 1905. The principal in charge of the work was DeRoy S. Fero. At that time, the general accountant for the Company was John Franklin Forbes, who came with it in 1902. Forbes was born March 24, 1876 in Wilmington, California, and graduated from the University of California. Mr. Fero was very much impressed with Forbes and suggested that Forbes should go into practice for himself as a Public Accountant. Forbes did this in 1906, shortly before the earthquake and fire of April 18, 1906. The disaster proved beneficial to Forbes as accounting assistance was necessary for many organizations because of the destruction of records. Forbes also was engaged for special work by the United Railways of San Francisco, this being his largest client.

Mr. Fero kept in touch with Forbes during his auditing work for Haskins & Sells in San Francisco, and in 1912 the agreement was reached for the consolidation of the practices.

Mr. Forbes was the Managing Partner in San Francisco from 1912 to 1919, and District Manager of the Pacific Coast Offices and Shanghai to 1926, when he went to the Executive Office in New York in an Advisory and Management capacity. He became one of the Senior Partners in the Firm, but in 1930 he wished to return to San Francisco. He became Resident Partner there again. The change did not prove to be as happy a one as he had hoped, and in 1932 he resigned from the Firm to enter into a more personal practice as Consulting Accountant and Economist. This soon led him to resume the practice of accounting under the name of John F. Forbes & Co. which he continued until his death on July 8, 1965. The firm of John F. Forbes & Co. continues to practice.

5

World War I—The Technical Procedure Department—John R. Wildman—Training Classes—Cash Verification—Internal Control Questionnaires—Tests of Transactions—General Questionnaire—Service Classification

The Firm at the beginning of World War I in 1914 consisted of Elijah W. Sells, Charles S. Ludlam, Homer A. Dunn, Howard B. Cook, Charles E. Morris, Arthur S. Vaughan, John F. Forbes, Leslie N. Simson, Edward Fuller, Peter White, and John N. Patton.

The period of the War was one of activity and growth. The year nineteen fifteen saw the addition of three new offices, Watertown (New York), Atlanta, and Denver. In Watertown on April 1, 1915, the Firm acquired and merged with its own the practice of Mr. C. E. Scoville, a former member for several years of the New York staff. Mr. Scoville remained as Manager of the Watertown Office. In Atlanta the office was opened on June 1, 1915, with L. C. Matthews as Manager. The Denver Office was opened on the same date with Mr. C. H. Banks as Manager.

Los Angeles followed on October 1, 1916, when the Firm acquired, and consolidated with its own, the practice of Mr. Frederick F. Hahn. Mr. Hahn continued with the Firm as Manager of the Los Angeles Office, becoming a partner in 1922. He was a broad gauged and highly skilled accountant with a most engaging personality, and developed a wide and deep acquaintance with influential businessmen in Los Angeles. These qualities, together with his sound judgment of men, resulted in building the practice in that city into one of the largest and most important in the Firm.

He was a keen golfer and an excellent though venturesome bridge and poker player. After a period of ill health arising from overwork and nervous tension, he made one trip abroad on a freighter with Mrs. Hahn, but only one for he was a confirmed and enthusiastic Californian

Frederick F. Hahn, a broad gauged and highly skilled accountant who laid the foundation for today's extensive Los Angeles practice of Haskins & Sells.

and found no other place nearly as attractive as California.

Notwithstanding the fact of the Great War, the demands upon the Firm made it necessary to open two new offices during the year nineteen seventeen—one in Seattle, June 1, 1917, and one in Detroit, July 2, 1917. Mr. P. C. Davis was appointed Manager of the Seattle Office; Mr. L. E. Palmer, Manager in Detroit.

During the War, many members of the organization served their Country in one capacity or another. Forty staff accountants were in active service. One of them, Captain Thomas V. Barb, of Baltimore, was cited and received the Croix de Guerre for "exceptional courage in sticking to his Battery and taking care of his men after having been badly wounded." Twelve served in civil capacity. Three members of the Firm gave their services to various war activities.

Mr. Ludlam went to France in November 1918 to take charge of the accounting between the United States and the Allied Governments. One of his staff was Lloyd L. Tompkins, who later became a partner. In April 1919 Mr. Ludlam again went abroad to serve in the capacity of accountant for the United States Liquidation Commission.

Mr. Dunn represented the Firm in directing the Bureau of Audits of the Alien Property Custodian's office. On this important work Mr. Dunn was in Washington slightly over a year.

In January 1918, when the American National Red Cross asked for help in putting its accounts in shape to be audited by the War Department, the Firm offered its service gratis as a contribution to the cause. One of the partners, Leslie N. Simson, spent several months in Washington, where under his direction the records for the six months ended December 31, 1917 showing receipts of $40,151,629.26 and disbursements of $35,452,546.06 were rewritten to make the audit possible.

The Firm carried employees engaged in service on either an honorary or effective payroll, according to the circumstances, and welcomed back all who desired to return after the close of the War.

Early in 1918 a special unit was organized in our Executive Office to give systematic attention to problems in the fields of technical research and professional training. This measure responded to needs already felt, and, as it proved, it also anticipated the larger needs which arose in constantly increasing degree throughout the 1920s. The problems to be dealt with were in part directly connected with the major expansion of our own practice in volume and geographical spread.

In no less important degree they also reflected the acute growing pains of the profession as a whole.

In the twenties the capacities of the profession were taxed to the fullest by the demands of a furiously expanding national economy. Industrial activity, after a sharp decline in 1920, rose to new peacetime heights; producers and consumers alike prospered beyond all previous experience, plant construction boomed; the securities markets absorbed huge amounts of new capital issues; investment trusts emerged from a negligible position in finance to one of large importance; and the process of large-scale consolidation of corporations, quiescent for the previous fifteen years, again played a conspicuous part in the evolution of business, notably through the formation of great holding companies in the public utility field.

An indication of what all this meant to the profession was to be found in the swarms of young candidates who crowded the CPA examination rooms. The ratio of experienced to inexperienced practicing accountants was dropping; while on the technical side the profession awoke to the realization that it had, on the whole, done little in the way of codifying principles and practices. This was particularly true of its practicing members. In the field of accounting theory their academic associates, such as Professor William Morse Cole of Harvard and Professor Henry Rand Hatfield of California, had made valuable contributions. For the making of a well-rounded body of authoritative professional guides, particularly on the auditing side, these had to be substantially prepared by practitioners having first hand contact with a wealth of case material of constantly spreading ramifications.

Our own research and training unit when organized in 1918 was headed by John R. Wildman. Mr. Wildman, born in 1878, after a brief period at Yale University entered Government service at the time of the Spanish American War. He later became Disbursing Officer and Chief of the Division of Disbursements and Accounts for the Department of Education in Puerto Rico. In 1905 he wanted to return to the United States, and entered the employ of Haskins & Sells. He attended New York University, graduating in 1909 (cum laude) being awarded the Accounting Prize. He received a part-time appointment as Professor of Accounting in 1909. This developed into full-time activity in New York University, and resigning from Haskins & Sells he became head of the Department of Accounting, where he did much to organize and develop education in accounting. There were few satisfactory text books

John R. Wildman, a founder of the forerunner of the American Accounting Association and head of New York University's Accounting Department, organized the H&S research and training unit in 1918 and initiated important technical procedures.

on accounting and Mr. Wildman wrote "Introduction to Accounting," "Principles of Accounting," "Principles of Auditing," and "Principles of Cost Accounting" for classroom use.

He together with five other professors of accounting, Fayette H. Elwell, University of Wisconsin, Charles C. Huntington, Ohio State University, Martin J. Shugrue, Massachusetts Institute of Technology, John E. Treleven, University of Texas, and John Bauer, Princeton University, founded in 1916 the American Association of University Instructors in Accounting (later the American Accounting Association). Mr. Wildman was elected the first President at the first meeting in Columbus, Ohio, December 28, 1916, which was also attended by the founders and among others, Carl A. Saliers, Yale University, Henry R. Hatfield, University of California, Hiram T. Scovill, University of Illinois, David Friday, New York University, and John C. Duncan, University of Cincinnati.

On January 16, 1918, Mr. Wildman returned to the Firm on a part-time basis to undertake the development of professional training. It became evident that it was a full-time task, and he became a partner December 1, 1918. Associated with him were William H. Bell and Edmund C. Gause, who had been with Haskins & Sells since 1909, and Edward A. Kracke, who had come to the Firm in 1912. Initial attention was centered on the training of recruits. The program was, however, steadily broadened and material was made available to our entire organization which represented the fruits of extensive reexamination of traditional auditing practices and critical scrutiny of the contemporary evolution in concepts of accounting and reporting. The professional training work was expanded in 1924 to the Technical Procedure Department.

Training classes were formed for the instruction of junior accountants through lectures by qualified persons and the study of specially prepared texts. These were the first steps in a fruitful evolution in personnel policies which came to include measures for ensuring a constant replenishment of the vitality of the organization and long-range maintenance of its standards through the annual enrollment of specially selected men.

In technical research, the program contemplated fresh emphasis on some of the elementals of auditing. The earliest studies were concerned with the verification of cash and its relationship to the broader subject of internal check and control. Analyses were made of

Mr. Sells and Mr. Ludlam, with Miss Bolles, the Executive Office Secretary, between them, lend their support to the Firm's first professional training class in the summer of 1920. Next to Mr. Sells are Homer Dunn and then John Wildman, who organized the course.

some one hundred and fifty cases of embezzlement, effected by manipulation of accounts or collusion of personnel, which had been turned up in the actual execution of audit engagements. The distribution of these case histories in 1926, along with a set of generalized conclusions and procedural guides, had immediate value in the field work of our organization, and in assuring a consistent practice of impressing upon clients, when needed, the importance of improving their organizational setup or otherwise strengthening their procedures against internal fraud.

The observation of inventories and the confirmation of accounts receivable were emphasized and required. In the middle twenties a New York bank contemplated bringing a suit against Haskins & Sells for several million dollars for a loss it suffered on a loan to a department store. It appeared that the President of the department store had diverted merchandise to a corporation which was owned by himself, and for that reason refused to permit us to observe inventory quantities on hand. We had qualified our certificate even though not required to do so by the professional standards then in existence. Mr. Wildman had asked the bankers if they read our certificate contained in our report. The bankers admitted they had not. When they read our certificate, they admitted they had no grounds for a case against us.

One of the innovations resulting from Mr. Wildman's orderly mind was the Service Classification, which was promulgated to the organization in November 1925. It divided accounting service into thirteen classes with the result of clarifying the mind of everyone in the organization as to the type of service undertakings, affording a basis for definite understanding with clients as to what each type contemplated, and when referred to in reports left no doubt as to the service performed. It was of great technical and administrative value to the Firm and indeed to the profession. The service classification recommended by Haskins & Sells was approved by formal action by several state societies of certified public accountants and in October 1930 by the American Society of Certified Public Accountants (later merged with the American Institute of Accountants).

This was followed by Cash Questionnaires, Programs for Verification of Cash Transactions, and General Questionnaires.

The principle had long been recognized by the profession in a general sort of way, that adequate internal control was an essential pillar of an independent audit of the affairs of the modern business enterprise. Test audits were the only form of examination which could be made without excessive cost. The chief practical problem of every audit conducted on the principle of testing and sampling was whether and in what degree systems of internal check and control were effective and what should be the manner and extent of the necessary audit tests.

Profession-wide the subject of internal control had undoubtedly received in the aggregate a great deal of consideration by individual accountants as the problem arose in practice, job by job. But it plainly called for more systematic analysis on a broad base and an attempt to reach more comprehensive conclusions. The outlines of the problem needed to be sharpened and its implications clarified, if they were not to be obscured by more conspicuous questions of accounting theory then at issue, while businessmen, governmental bodies, academic authorities, and accountants vigorously debated the many-sided subject of properly distinguishing between capital and income, and other controversial matters such as the setting of reasonable standards of materiality for facts requiring disclosure in financial reports.

In our own organization a comprehensive study of internal control was made, and after a preliminary period of trial a standard H. & S. Form of Internal Control Questionnaire was devised for use as an aid in surveying clients' systems and for incorporation in audit working papers. A second exhibit embraced three model programs of Tests of Transactions, the choice in the use of which by the partner or principal in supervisory charge of the engagement depended on the conclusions to which his system investigation pointed. Two other model working papers were originated at about the same time—a Program for Verification of Cash Balances and a General Questionnaire. Since that time, these four standard working papers have been revised from year to year as experience has indicated to be desirable.

Paralleling the task of research and current distribution of new material there was undertaken the collation, revision, and codification of a large amount of material contained in existing files of circular letters of information and instruction. This work eventuated in a comprehensive Technical Procedure Manual, now Audit Practice Manual, in which much material, old and new, was systematized and brought into a form facilitating reference. This manual is being continually revised to keep it abreast of new developments.

The program of codification of technical practices, the bare outlines of which have been set out as above, was in no way intended to curb original thinking or discourage self-reliance on the part of any member of our organization. Nor did it have that result, even though on important matters of principle consistency of procedures throughout the organization reflecting the weight of opinion was required. The benefits of centralized research, able to draw upon extensive sources of information and experience, were expected to be large; and so it proved. Not least among them was the facility given to every accountant of reaching informed and balanced conclusions of his own on any one of a wide range of subjects in which his personal experience may not have been broad enough to satisfy an inquiring mind.

6

*Men who cooperated with John R. Wildman—William H. Bell—
Edward A. Kracke—College Recruitment Program—
Weldon Powell—Ralph S. Johns—Haskins & Sells Bulletin*

The two partners who collaborated most closely with John R. Wildman in the development of technical procedures were William H. Bell and Edward A. Kracke.

William Hansell Bell was one of the many young men in the early part of the burgeoning twentieth century, the direction of whose life was the result of contact with a discerning man. He was born in Uxbridge, Ontario, October 1, 1883, the son of a clergyman. The family moved to New York State in 1895. Bell, to go to High School in Springville boarded with a farmer near the town, milking the cows and doing other farm chores for his board. Some years after graduation from High School he was employed in the office of Stromberg Carlson Telephone Manufacturing Company, when Haskins & Sells made an audit of that Company with Charles E. Morris in charge. Morris was impressed with Bell, and he suggested that Bell take up public accounting. This led to Bell coming to New York to enroll as a student in the evening division of New York University School of Commerce, Accounts and Finance, graduating in 1910 with the degree of B.C.S. cum laude. In 1909 he received a position as assistant accountant in the Report Department of Haskins & Sells.

His strong drive for professional status continued and he took and passed the New York State CPA examination in 1910, became a member of the New York State Society of CPAs in 1911, of the American Society of Certified Public Accountants in 1912, and of the American Institute of Accountants in 1916.

In the Firm his capacity for work and his technical ability were quickly recognized. He became Assistant Manager in Baltimore in 1915,

William Hansell Bell, author of definitive accounting references and craftsman with language, collaborated with John R. Wildman in pioneering technical procedures and training methods.

Manager of the St. Louis Office in 1917, and a partner in 1918. He returned to New York in 1918 to work with Mr. Wildman in professional training and technical procedure areas. Mr. Bell was a highly skilled technician, a precisionist, with a wide ranging and keen mind on accounting and auditing procedures, and an authority on English usage.

He was active in professional societies, serving on boards and committees. He also wrote papers on accounting matters and a number of books: "Accountants' Reports" in 1921, "Auditing" in 1924, with revised editions by Bell and Johns in 1941 and 1952, and "Accountants' Working Papers" by Bell and Palmer in 1923 with a subsequent edition, revised by Ralph S. Johns in 1950.

Edward Augustus Kracke was an unusual and distinctive accountant. He was born in New York in 1882 in a family with a strong sense of public service. He was educated in the New York schools and at Harvard, where he majored in classical and other languages—giving him the facility he later needed and used in French and German; and the illumination of his speech with Latin and Greek quotations. He completed the four years study at Harvard in three years, graduating in 1904 with the degree of Bachelor of Arts, cum laude, in the class of Franklin Delano Roosevelt. This basic education he expanded and developed with wide and deep reading in history, economics, and literature.

After graduation, he tried restlessly fields of banking, finance, and real estate, coming to a conviction that his field of preference was in public accounting. When he was thirty years old in 1912, he joined Haskins & Sells. He was tempted many times by offers of important and more lucrative positions in business, but consistently refused them, saying that he was in public accounting to stay.

He rose rapidly in the Firm of Haskins & Sells, becoming Associate Manager in the Firm's Chicago Office in 1918, Manager in 1920, and a partner in 1921. After the First World War, the reconstruction of Europe's industry brought American financiers into active participation and Mr. Kracke was in Europe from 1924 to 1930, rendering important accounting service in connection with financing in Germany, France, Italy, and Poland and in developing the practice of Haskins & Sells through its offices in London, Berlin, and Paris. There were years of unremitting work under most difficult conditions and under constant tensions.

He returned from Europe in 1930 and plunged into technical

work for his Firm, giving attention to some of the Firm's most important engagements and also developing technical procedures for accounting work. This was the time in the profession in the United States when new views and new procedures were revolutionizing the profession, when the New York Stock Exchange was becoming more and more conscious of the need for better and more complete information for investors, when the banks through the association of bank credit men were pressing for clearer, more comprehensive statements for bank credit, when the Securities and Exchange Commission was coming into being and into a vital position in accounting accuracy and disclosure in reporting. It was therefore a time when Mr. Kracke's background, experience, wide vision, and keen mind could make great contributions to the profession. As one of the by-products of his activity he started for his Firm in 1933 a Statistical Survey of the certificates in 500 published reports of 1932 with the reproductions of many of the certificates. This was continued by Haskins & Sells until 1946, when it was turned over to the American Institute of Accountants, becoming their "Accounting Trends and Techniques" now in its 23rd edition.

Another by-product was his work on inventory valuation. He served as Chairman of the original Inventory Committee of the American Institute of Accountants which collaborated with the American Petroleum Institute on the subject of inventories over the years 1933 to 1936, and reported the "last in, first out" basis as an acceptable method of inventory valuation for certain industries. He subsequently served as a member of the Accounting Procedure Committee of the American Institute of Accountants and in that Committee devoted particular time to inventory valuation as Chairman of a subcommittee on that subject. In 1939 he served in an advisory capacity to the Treasury Department in connection with revising the income tax law upon the subject of inventory valuation in respect of "last in, first out" procedure. When the "last in, first out" method came up in the Canadian courts, Mr. Kracke's able testimony was one of the most important factors in the recognition by the court of the basis.

His intense interest in the development of accounting techniques was also evident when he was a member of the Committee in 1934, 1935, and 1936 which revised the Federal Reserve Board pamphlet of Accountants Reports. He was also the draftsman of the Tentative Statement on Auditing Standards, while on the American Institute of Accountants Committee on Auditing Procedure. This statement has

Edward Augustus Kracke, politically a witty and erudite conservative but in technical matters a revolutionary, who helped to modernize the Firm's procedures, placing it in the forefront of the profession.

since become the bible of independent auditors. Mr. Kracke believed strongly that good professional organizations were vital to the life and growth of the profession and he demonstrated this belief in his service to these professional organizations. He became a member of the American Society of Certified Public Accountants and of the American Institute of Accountants early in his career. In the American Institute of Accountants he was on the Council and a member of the Executive Committee from 1943 to 1949 and his committee service was on twenty-two committees, an amazing record of activity. In the New York State Society of Certified Public Accountants, he was a director for four years and President in 1948, and his service at various times on seventeen committees of the Society was outstanding.

He was also active in the New Jersey Society of Certified Public Accountants, in the Chamber of Commerce of the United States, and in the American Accounting Association, in which he was Vice President in 1946.

Over his whole life he had a keen interest in public affairs, and he was a person of strong opinions on national and political matters. His preoccupation with professional activities did not give him very much time for active participation in national activities except through his professional associations. However, his later work for the American Institute of Accountants after the Second World War was on Committees relating to Federal Government Accounting, and as Chairman of the Committee on Cooperation with the Congressional Appropriations Committees. This led him into close touch with Senator Byrd and Congressman Taber. Always a person of strong and deep convictions, he threw himself into this phase of national activity, served as a member of both Hoover Commissions, and as an adviser to the Maritime Commission. His work in public areas plus his long and valuable services to his profession resulted in the award in 1947 for outstanding service to the New York State Society of Certified Public Accountants and the award in 1948 by the American Institute of Accountants for "Outstanding Service."

His interest in his profession and in national life never flagged until his death in 1960.

Edward Kracke was much more than a highly skilled accountant with dedication to his profession, his Firm, and to the best interests of his Country. He was a fascinating and great human being. There were many personal facets—his firmly fixed views of personal and national integrity, his belief in hard work and his demonstration of it, his conservative, perhaps ultra conservative views, his erudition, his philological competence, his rhetorical fireworks, his pixyish sense of humor, and his mastery of the art of punning were all a part of him. Pervading all of his life were his warm affection for his friends, his willingness and even eagerness to "go the second Mile" for them, and his dedicated devotion to his family with his deep consciousness of how much he owed to them for his accomplishments and his happiness.

Few men had more richness in spirit, wide range of accomplishment, had given more to their business associates and to their professions and few will stay as deeply and as long and as affectionately in the minds and hearts of those who knew him.

It was these two men (Bell and Kracke) who with Mr. Wildman revolutionized and modernized the technical procedures of the Firm placing it in the forefront of the profession in these matters.

Under Mr. Wildman's guidance a program was commenced of recruitment from colleges and universities of graduates who had majored in accounting. The first of these was Weldon Powell from the University of Illinois. He was born in Logansport, Indiana January 4, 1903, the son of Dr. Jehu and Christine Markert Powell. Dr. Powell's ancestors had settled in the Logansport area in the 1820s just after the lands around it had been acquired from the Miami and Pottawattomie Indians. Dr. Powell was a practicing physician, but also active in community affairs, being Republican County Chairman, a member of the City Council, and a presidential elector in 1896 (the election of William McKinley). Both of the Powells were widely read in American historical, moral and religious classics. Their interest and concern as to his education explain Weldon Powell's facility in writing and his clarity and precision in thinking.

He attended schools in Logansport and, although his father died in January 1918, he was able to enter the University of Indiana in September 1918. Learning of the courses in accountancy at the University of Illinois he transferred there in 1919, his mother giving up her home in Logansport and moving to Champaign to make the change possible. He graduated in 1922 with a B.S. in Accountancy, with the award of "Final Honors." Desiring to continue his accounting studies he received a position as Assistant in Accountancy, and received his degree of M.S. in Accountancy in 1923, submitting a thesis on "Some Principles in Accounting for No-Par-Value Capital Stock," which was an exhaustive study of the development and legal status in all of the States, a document of 155 pages showing a clear and logical grasp of the subject and foreshadowing the thorough and meticulous handling of any matter in which he was interested.

In the classes, when Powell was teaching, were Andrew Barr (later Chief Accountant of the Securities and Exchange Commission) and John W. Queenan.

He enjoyed teaching and took a full-time position for the college year of 1923-1924 as Assistant in Accountancy at a salary of $1,400 a year. The failure of the University to promise him a salary of $1,700 for his second year led him to seek employment with a firm of accountants, a desire which he brought to the attention of Professor Scovill of the University of Illinois.

John R. Wildman, who was in charge of Professional Training at Haskins & Sells, was then seeking young men from the Universities for training in accountancy at Haskins & Sells. Wildman had been head of the Department of Accounting at New York University School of Commerce, Accounts and Finance, and through the American Association of University Instructors in Accounting had come to know very well Hiram T. Scovill of the University of Illinois.

At a meeting of the American Association of University Instructors in Accounting at Urbana, Wildman's attention was drawn to Weldon Powell's thesis on "Some Principles in Accounting for No-Par-Value Capital Stock" and its logic and clarity appealed to him. It was natural for Professor Scovill to speak well of Weldon Powell, and as a result Wildman offered Powell a position with Haskins & Sells in New York. Powell accepted and was given the post of Junior Assistant Accountant for the professional training staff on June 16, 1924 at $35 a week, essentially the salary at which he would have remained with the University of Illinois as a teacher. In the Technical Procedure Department he assisted Mr. Wildman in connection with the Haskins & Sells Bulletin, and in the development of technical procedures.

Early in 1927 Mr. Wildman spent four months in New Orleans in connection with an examination of the Guaranty Plan Corporation and in testimony as to an embezzlement in the Company. Mr. Powell was with him as his first practical audit work. In 1928 he was assigned to Newark for further practical training, and in 1930 became Manager, and in 1934 a Partner. He was then transferred to Los Angeles.

He returned to New York in 1947 to the Executive Office, where

Weldon Powell was a giant among accounting technicians in the profession and the Firm. Organizer and first chairman of the Accounting Principles Board, he was also a cultivated patron of music.

he gave attention to many important engagements and to the development and improvement of the technical work of the Firm. He was universally recognized as one of the leaders of the profession in technical matters.

He was active in the profession, holding CPA Certificates in 25 States, and serving on many committees of the American Institute of Certified Public Accountants, as well as on the Council of the Institute. One of his major accomplishments was the organization of the Accounting Principles Board. He was awarded posthumously in 1970 the Institute's Gold Medal for distinguished service to the profession.

Mr. Powell wrote extensively on technical accounting subjects and made many addresses both in the United States and abroad. His University of Illinois thesis was expanded into a book—coauthored by John R. Wildman "Capital Stock Without Par Value," published in 1928. It remained a classic in its field.

Weldon and his wife Mary (the niece of John R. Wildman) had wide interests outside of the profession.

The deep interest of the Powells in music was evident in many ways—in the Metropolitan Opera, which they attended regularly, and where he was a member of the Board of Directors of the Metropolitan Opera Association; in the Metropolitan National Council, where he was chairman of the Administrative Committee; in the Opera Club of which he was a Director; in the Manhattan School of Music, where he was a trustee; and in the University Club of New York, where he was a member of its Council and chairman of its Music Committee. In the Powells' home, music was a part of their life. They installed a superb hi-fi system with two loud speakers in their living room concealed by highly decorative screens. They had a collection of over a thousand fine records, practically all of them classical instrumental, symphonic and operatic, and practically at all times, whether entertaining guests or alone, music was heard softly.

One of the Powells' hobbies was the collection of antique glass paperweights. It started through the purchase in 1950 by Mary Powell of a small inexpensive paperweight in the flea market in Paris as a present to Weldon. It intrigued him and he commenced to buy paperweights in the United States, and later in London and Paris. He collected these steadily over a ten year period building up a group of 106 paperweights at a cost of about $26,500. They were beautifully displayed in two glass shelved niches in the living room at the Powell apartment at 2 East 70th Street, and was a highly regarded collection by paperweight experts.

When they were sold at auction at the Plaza Art Galleries on January 13, 1966, they brought $60,000.

Another of the Powells' passions was for travel. Their first trip abroad was in 1950 on what was basically a business trip to visit the plants and offices of General Motors Corporation in Europe. This covered England, Portugal, Spain, France, Belgium, Holland, Denmark, Sweden, Finland, Germany, and Switzerland. The trip proved so fascinating and delightful that they made many more trips to Europe. In 1956 they visited the Far East, and in 1965 spent ten weeks in Africa.

In addition to his hobby of collecting paperweights, Weldon Powell was an enthusiastic and competent photographer. He equipped himself with fine cameras and lenses and took great pains in taking pictures. They were made on all of his trips abroad and in the process he accumulated more than 7,500 colored transparent mounted slides, every one of which was marked as to the place and date on which the picture was taken. They were then organized into Kodak volumes by countries. His work was remarkably good judging by the slides he retained. How many unsatisfactory ones he destroyed is not known. These slides were examined after his death by another able amateur photographer, his partner, Ralph S. Johns, and were distributed to Veterans Homes, Children's Homes, Old Folks Homes, and Hospitals.

Over all of their life together Weldon and Mary had the faculty of making warm and lasting friends. They enjoyed people, especially those with common interests, such as Weldon's Firm of Haskins & Sells, professional societies, clients, music, church, clubs, and hobbies.

The death of Weldon Powell and his wife in an automobile accident on October 23, 1965 was a great loss to the Firm and to their many friends.

The second college graduate employed for the Technical Procedure Department by Mr. Wildman was Ralph S. Johns, who was born in Oak Park, Illinois July 8, 1904, and after attending Oak Park schools entered the University of Illinois September 1921, receiving his B.S. in Accountancy with high honors in 1925 and his M.S. in 1926 with a thesis on "The Natural Business Year." He obtained his Illinois CPA Certificate in 1925. He was employed July 15, 1926 in New York and assisted Mr. Wildman in professional training matters.

Ralph S. Johns' work for his profession, extending over 36 years and covering a wide variety of activities, is one of the outstanding examples of dedicated service to the profession of accountancy.

He was transferred to Newark December 1, 1927, securing his New Jersey CPA Certificate in 1929, and his New York CPA Certificate in 1932. Mr. Johns came to the New York Broad Street Office in 1938, becoming a member of the Firm June 1, 1943. In 1950 he was transferred to Chicago, becoming Senior Partner in that office in 1951.

Mr. Johns was most active in professional societies—serving the New Jersey State Society on its Board of Trustees, Member and Chairman of various committees, and Vice President and President; the Illinois State Society as a Member of the Board of Directors, on thirteen committees (five of them as Chairman); the American Institute of Certified Public Accountants on thirteen committees (six of them as Chairman), as a Member of Council and on the Trial Board; the Illinois Board of Examiners in Accountancy (as Chairman); the National Association of State Boards of Accountancy as Director, Vice President, and President; and numerous other professional services. His work for his profession extended over 36 years and, covering a wide variety of activities, is one of the most outstanding examples of dedicated service to the profession of accountancy. As a firm believer in community activity he served the Union League Club of Chicago as Treasurer and First Vice President; the Union League Foundation for Boys Clubs as Trustee, Treasurer, and Vice President; the Union League Civic and Arts Foundation as Director and President; the Village of Wilmette as Member of the Board of Trustees; as Member of the Board of Auditors of the New Trier Township; as Chairman of the Board of Trustees of the Wilmette Baptist Church; as Member of the Board of Trustees of the Northern Baptist Theological Seminary; as Member of the Board of Directors of the University of Illinois Foundation; and as President of the University of Illinois Alumni Association.

Early in Mr. Johns' career he made examinations of universities and became deeply interested not only in their accounting, but in the treatment of their funds. This led, thirty years ago, to planning for the pooling of Endowment Funds and a paper on this subject by him appeared in the Journal of Accountancy in 1939. He continued to study, discuss, and write on College Accounting and Administration, and from 1960 to 1968 served on the Revision Committee for Volumes I and II of College and University Business Administration of the National Association of College and University Business Officers. In the Journal of Accountancy for March 1969 he collaborated with Howard A. Withey in an article to discuss the most significant changes in the revision issued by the Committee.

His investigations broadened to include most non-profit organizations, and he wrote and talked about their accounting. He was Special Consultant to the American Hospital Associations Committee on Accounting and Business Practices from 1958 to 1964.

He is recognized as one of the leading authorities on the accounting for college and other non-profit organizations.

Another subject to which he gave much thought was that of Professional Ethics. He was on the Committee on Professional Ethics of the Illinois Society of Certified Public Accountants from 1955 to 1958 serving as Chairman for two years. This was followed by five years from 1962 to 1967 on the Ethics Committee of the American Institute of Certified Public Accountants, the last three as Chairman, when he did much in the codification and interpretation of the subject. Logically on the termination of his work on the Ethics Committee, he was appointed as a member of the Trial Board of the Institute.

In the technical accounting field he was the author with William H. Bell of "Auditing," and with Bell and Leslie E. Palmer of "Accountants' Working Papers," and contributed many articles to the Journal of Accountancy on these matters.

Another sphere of activity over twenty years has been his Alma Mater, the University of Illinois. He held all of the offices in the Illini Club of Chicago from Director to Chairman, Director and President of the Alumni Assn., and a Director of the University of Illinois Foundation.

All of this was while he was intensively engaged in practice, in managing very successfully the Chicago Office and developing men. Among the personnel brought into the Chicago Office during the eighteen years when he was partner in charge of the office, there are twenty-six men who are now partners in thirteen different offices.

His service with the Union League Club Civic and Arts Foundation led to an active interest in painting. Among his hobbies, are photography, in which he is skilled, and paperweights of which he has a fine collection.

Since Mr. Wildman commenced the practice of drawing men from the colleges and universities, many thousands of graduates have been started by Haskins & Sells on their professional careers.

Another of Mr. Wildman's conceptions was the Haskins & Sells Bulletin. This was to be largely the organ of the Professional Training Department to bring to the attention of the staff technical developments in accounting, auditing, and reporting. To enliven it some personal items were included, as were book reviews, library additions, and organization changes. The first issue was dated March 15, 1918, and the Bulletin continued—generally on a monthly basis—until January 1932. Reading its issues over these fourteen years shows the technical changes and improvements in the profession, and much of the history of the Firm in that period. Mr. Wildman in the earlier years of the Bulletin had the active help of Weldon Powell, Ralph S. Johns and John W. Queenan.

There were articles on practical audit matters: Cash, receivables, inventories and inventory valuation, depreciation, actual and contingent liabilities, reserves, surplus, recurring charges, Federal taxes, balance sheet audits, and audit working papers. Report matters were carefully covered: Preparation and writing of reports, including grammatical construction and the use of words, comments, footnotes, qualifications, and comparative statements.

Many specific subjects were covered in accounting for: Foreign exchange, trust companies, oil producers, milk distribution, paper mills, mining, holding companies, investment trusts, social agencies, governments, and general items such as mechanical devices, Natural Business Year, and budgeting.

Professional subjects were dealt with under: Ethics, ideals, negligence, service classification, and qualifications of assistants and in-charge accountants. General reports came in from abroad and so there were articles on London, France, Cuba, Europe, China, Scandinavia, Germany, and South America.

With the long and deep interest of Mr. Wildman in no-par and treasury stock, there were ten articles dealing with various phases of these subjects—the last one an article by Mr. Wildman on "The Capital Adjustment Theory of Treasury Stock."

In 1930 and 1931, as the field of technical subjects had been very well covered in the past, it became difficult to get new and fresh articles and the Bulletin was made a quarterly. Mr. Wildman's health and preoccupation with other matters also added to the problem of producing the Bulletin, so that with the abstruse and highly theoretical article on Treasury Stock, which took up the whole of the January 1932 Bulletin, it was decided to discontinue it. During its existence, it had served a very useful purpose in acquainting the staff with sound and helpful ideas in accounting and auditing.

7

*The Executive Office—Arthur H. Carter—
Mergers 1919-1923—Arthur B. Foye*

On May 1, 1919 the Executive Office of the organization was made effective and the Executive Office was opened at 469 Fifth Avenue, New York.

Prior to this time and for a number of years, several of the Firm members had gradually been devoting a large part of their time to directing the administration of offices other than New York. As the offices increased in number, the necessity for such guidance became more apparent. It was also seen that if the same kind and quality of service were to be rendered to clients, regardless of where such clients might be, or the office to which they might apply, and provision were to be made for expansion, refinements in the organization must be effected.

The Executive Office was therefore established, because of the desire to separate it physically from the New York practice office so as to emphasize its existence. It was also thought that such measure would help to give a better perspective of the organization as a whole to those who were to be responsible for its administration.

The Executive Office moved to 37 West 39th Street, when that building was purchased in 1920, and remained there until the sale of the building in 1925. The office then moved to 30 Broad Street, to 15 Broad Street in 1928, to 67 Broad Street in 1937, and to 2 Broadway in 1959.

The opening of the Executive Office in 1919 coincided with the entrance into the organization of Arthur Hazleton Carter. He came with Haskins & Sells to give attention to Firm expansion and development.

Haskins & Sells owes much of its position today to Arthur H. Carter, whose administrative skill as managing partner guided the Firm through the Depression years of the 1930s. He achieved distinction both as a soldier and as an accountant.

To few men is the opportunity given to serve their country with distinction as both soldier and civilian. Arthur H. Carter was one of this special breed. He was born in Hillsboro, Kansas on January 6, 1884. After graduating from High School in Marion, Kansas, he secured a nomination to West Point. Because he was too young, the Academy would not take him that year, and he attended Braden's School at Highland Falls, a preparatory school for West Point. He was then admitted to the Academy in 1901 at the age of 17, graduating in 1905 as a Second Lieutenant in the Field Artillery with the degree of Bachelor of Science. According to the West Point Howitzer he developed from a shy, bashful youth to a man of brawn and nerve. His first post as a Second Lieutenant was with the Field Artillery at Fort Leavenworth, Kansas. In 1908 he was sent to the Philippines as a First Lieutenant and served three years at Camp Stotsenberg and Fort William McKinley and as aide-de-camp to General Ramsay D. Potts, Commander of the Department of Luzon in the Philippines during the governorship of General Leonard Wood. It was there in the winter of 1908-09 that he met Marjorie Sells, who had accompanied her father, Elijah Watt Sells, on a mission to investigate the keeping of accounts in the Government departments in the Philippines. They were married in New York in 1910. He came back to the service later that year to serve at posts in Kansas, first at Fort Leavenworth and then at Fort Riley, and was ordered to militia duty in Minnesota, Ohio, Pennsylvania, Michigan, and Wisconsin before again serving as General Potts aide-de-camp in Chicago in 1911, after General Wood became Chief of Staff for Secretary of War Henry L. Stimson.

Both Lieutenant and Mrs. Carter were skilled in horsemanship and when Secretary Stimson rode on maneuvers in Wyoming with his wife and her niece, the Carters were asked to accompany them.

From 1912 to 1915 he was stationed at Fort Meyer, Virginia, when he resigned to enter banking and farming in nearby Leesburg. He remained close to the Army all his life, however, and answered the call to duty in both World Wars.

Although the Field Artillery was his first love, when he returned to active duty in 1917 it was as a Major of Ordnance. In 1918, when he became a Colonel, he was transferred at his own request to the Field Artillery and was commissioned a Lieutenant Colonel. That summer he went to Camp Zachary Taylor, Kentucky, where he organized the Field Artillery Central Officers Training School, and administered that facility until the end of the War. Always looking for ways to combine service and education, this was a particularly agreeable assignment for him. He was awarded the Distinguished Service Medal "for exceptionally meritorious and conspicuous service" for his work in establishing and running the school. His training program for young artillery officers is described in the book he wrote with Archibald V. Arnold, "Field Instruction." The program involved 10,000 students, graduating 3,540 officers.

At the close of the War, Colonel Carter asked to be relieved of his command. Mr. Sells had followed his career closely and recognizing his administrative ability brought him into Haskins & Sells April 1, 1919, where his earlier training was to stand him in good stead. He applied himself assiduously to his new profession, became a CPA, and in 1922 was admitted to the Firm. He was designated as senior executive partner in 1927 at the age of 43 and became managing partner in 1930. His administrative skill guided the Firm through the Depression years of the 1930s, from which it emerged with a sounder financial structure than before. He had earlier established the valuable relationship with Deloitte, Plender, Griffiths & Co., which has since resulted in the successful handling of much of our foreign work and in the establishment of DPH&S offices throughout the world. During his twenty years as senior partner the number of Firm partners increased from 29 to 88. To him more than to any other person the Firm owes its policy that a partner shall have the close and intimate supervision of each engagement.

Over the years, Colonel Carter held many prominent positions in the accounting fraternity. He was a vice president of the American Institute of CPAs, a member of its Committee on Accounting procedure, and for three terms president of the New York State Society of CPAs. He served as president of the National Association of Accountants, where he is remembered for the Carter Trophy he donated for the chapter showing greatest improvement in its competitive standing.

His services in World War II are set forth in Chapter 10.

Arthur Carter had a boyhood ambition to become a doctor but it was because medical education was beyond his means that he went to West Point. He retained his interest in medicine all his life, founding a hospital in Leesburg, Virginia and heading a building fund drive for the hospital in his home town of Greenwich, Connecticut. He was elected to the Board of Governors of Good Samaritan Hospital in West Palm

Beach, Florida in 1949 and was President of the Board from 1952 to his death in 1965. He was deeply interested in the welfare and services of the Hospital, and also conducted its administration so that it operated without a deficit.

He always led an active outdoor life, riding, golfing, hunting, and fishing. Together he and Mrs. Carter spent summers salmon fishing on the Kedgewick and Restigouche rivers in New Brunswick. Winston Ferguson, his companion and guide on the river for many years, remembers him as "a great fisherman and hunter . . . who will be missed in the area for a long time."

Colonel Carter had a reputation for saying "No" with considerable firmness and regularity, but this seemed often just a testing process. If you were able to back up your ideas, they could pass muster with him. Mr. Queenan remembered, when still a principal and in charge of the Newark Office, he went to Colonel Carter to suggest moving the office to larger quarters. After his first unhesitating "No" and reasons why it was unnecessary and costly, Mr. Queenan brought out a floor plan which he "happened to have." Colonel Carter not only approved it, but instructed him to get new furniture for the new office. Mr. Coursen, who had taken Mr. Queenan in to see the Colonel, said as they left, "I never thought you'd get it."

Colonel Carter once remarked to his partners, "There is very little past in an organization, there is only a present and a future." The wisdom of that statement is indisputable, and yet the true character of a firm is built upon its history, much as a fine painting depends on the foundation of structure and composition. Haskins & Sells owes much of its position today to Arthur Carter.

In Haskins & Sells the first of Colonel Carter's assignments was firm expansion and development. His military experience had taken him to many parts of the Country and to the Far East, and helped by this knowledge in the years between 1919 and 1925 he made arrangements for a number of mergers:

1919	Henry J. Jumonville	New Orleans
1920	George R. Lamb	Cincinnati
1920	Grover C. Bland	Dallas
1920	Lawrence & Lawrence	Denver
1920	Hervey S. Champlin	Buffalo
1920	Stevenson & Carson	Shanghai

1921	Hollis, Tilton & Porte	Detroit
1921	Augustus Nickerson	Boston
1921	F. M. Weaver	Kansas City
1922	Archibald F. Wagner	Minneapolis
1923	C. Palmer Parker	Birmingham
1923	Wilfred L. Hagerty	Providence

This list of mergers appears impressive and while they did help to establish or strengthen offices in strategic cities, there were many difficulties in fitting them into the Haskins & Sells pattern. They did bring in some excellent partners, including Henry Jumonville in New Orleans, Spencer Stevenson in Shanghai and New York, Archibald Wagner in Minneapolis and Pittsburgh, and Ralph Hollis and Frederick Tilton in Detroit. In the year following the merger in Detroit, Ralph Hollis started for London to undertake the supervision of the European practice, but regrettably died on the ship going over. Frederick Tilton left the Firm in 1929 to become Third Assistant Postmaster General in charge of accounting, returning to Haskins & Sells in 1933.

The flow of American capital abroad after the War led to the opening of five more foreign offices: at Shanghai in 1919, Havana and Paris the following year, Berlin in 1924, and Manila in 1926. Further details of the expansion of our foreign practice are included in Chapter 13.

Back home, the much higher levels of industrial productivity led to the more than doubling of the roll of domestic offices by the opening of nineteen new locations: Boston in 1918; New Orleans and Philadelphia in 1919; Kansas City, Tulsa, Cincinnati, Dallas, Buffalo, and Salt Lake City in 1920; New York (uptown), Portland (Oregon), and Minneapolis in 1921; Newark in 1922; Birmingham, San Diego, and Providence in 1923; Brooklyn in 1925; and Jacksonville and Charlotte in 1926.

In 1928 and 1929 Mr. Ludlam's failing health kept him in Florida most of the time. Arthur B. Foye, whom John R. Wildman had brought into the organization in 1918, took over administrative duties with Colonel Carter.

Mr. Foye was born in Brooklyn, New York in 1893 and began his career as an instructor in accounting at New York University in 1915, the year after he received his Bachelor of Commercial Science degree magna cum laude from New York University's School of Commerce. He was also Assistant to John R. Wildman, then head of the Department

Arthur B. Foye was acting managing partner from 1942 to 1947 and managing partner from 1947 to 1956. He was president of the American Institute of Certified Public Accountants in 1953-54. He encouraged his partners to participate in other than professional affairs.

of Accounting. In 1916 he accompanied Professor Wildman to the first meeting in Columbus, Ohio of the American Association of University Instructors in Accounting—now the American Accounting Association. He became head of the Tax Department in 1920, and in 1923, the year he became a Certified Public Accountant in New York, he was made a partner in the Firm.

He was active in professional societies, having been Chairman of four standing committees of the American Institute of Certified Public Accountants, a member of its governing council, Executive Committee, and its Trial Board. In 1953 the Institute elected him President.

He was also active in the New York State Society of Certified Public Accountants, being Chairman of four committees and a member of ten other committees. He served as director and Vice President, and as President from 1956-1957.

He held Certificates in ten States and was a commissaire au comptes of France. Both the American Institute of Certified Public Accountants and the New York State Society of Certified Public Accountants gave him their Distinguished Service Awards. He is a member of the Ohio State University Accounting Hall of Fame.

In New York University he served as President of the School of Commerce Alumni Association and the General Alumni Federation, and Chairman of the Alumni Fund. He was a trustee of the University from 1952 to 1964. With Chancellor Henry Heald he was instrumental in establishing the Albert Gallatin Associates of the University, an organization of individual and corporate contributors that presents an annual award to a graduate or honorary alumnus of New York University who has rendered distinguished public service. Dr. Jonas Salk received the first Gallatin Medal in 1957. Mr. Foye served as first Chairman of the Gallatin Associates, and is now Honorary Chairman. He received the Madden Memorial Award, the University's Meritorius Service Medal, the New York University Alumni Federation Certificate of Honor, and the Arch and Square Award for service to the University.

In the post World War II years he served on four committees of United States Government foreign aid agencies. He was a member of the Public Advisory Committee for the China program of the Economic Cooperation Administration in 1948-49, of the Advisory Committee on Undeveloped Areas for the Mutual Security Agency in 1951-53, of the agency's survey group for Britain in 1953, and on the Task Force on Overseas Economic Operations of the Hoover Commission on

Organization of the Executive Branch of the Government in 1954-1956. For several years, he was a member of the United States National Commission for United Nations Economic and Social Council (UNESCO) and was Chairman of the Council's Eighth Annual Conference in New York in 1959.

In 1957-62 Mr. Foye was President of the Eighth International Congress, which after five years of organization work held its meeting in 1962 in New York with four thousand members of the profession in attendance from all parts of the free World (51 countries).

A strong believer in participation by accountants in other than professional affairs he encouraged the partners to also participate. Following his own precept Mr. Foye served as Vice Chairman of the International Economic Affairs Committee of the National Association of Manufacturers and attended its International Conferences in New York, Paris, and London. He is also a trustee of the United States Council of the International Chamber of Commerce. For thirteen years he was President of the Far East-America Council of Commerce and Industry. Among other things he was Treasurer for the Relief of the Philippines during the Second World War, and later helped found the African Affairs Society and the American Turkish Society. He was a director and member of the Executive Committee of the Asia Society in its formative period.

He was Chairman of the International Committee of the YMCA, and has been a member of the Finance Committee of the National Girl Scouts of America.

In his community he has been President of the YMCA, a director of the Valley Hospital, a member of the Board of Education, and helped establish the Community Chest. In New York he was for thirteen years Treasurer of St. Bartholomew's Church, where he is still an Honorary Vestryman.

8

The Miller Case

The postwar booms in the twenties brought much increased activity to accountants, but the collapse of these booms resulted in some serious problems for the accounting profession and the Firm. With corporations suffering financial reverses, the instigation of suits against directors of the companies and against the accountants who had given opinions on their financial statements became a lucrative field for certain lawyers. In 1927 there were indications that a New York accountant and a New York lawyer were trying to persuade preferred stockholders of G. L. Miller & Company, Inc. to bring a suit for damages against the partners of Haskins & Sells. G. L. Miller & Company, Inc. had been a client whose business consisted of underwriting bonds on real estate, usually on buildings to be constructed, acting as trustee under the mortgage indentures and selling the bonds to the public. The Firm made examinations for the years ended August 31, 1922, 1923, 1924 and 1925. A balance sheet as of August 31, 1925 was prepared giving effect to the proposed sale of $3,000,000 of 8% preferred stock. A note was appended to the balance sheet showing that the earnings for the year ended December 31, 1924 were in excess of 2½ times the dividends on the contemplated issue of preferred stock, and that the earnings for the eight months ended August 31, 1925 were in excess of 3 times the dividend requirements. The pro-forma balance sheet and earnings statement were used in the promotion of the sale of the preferred stock, which was sold between October 24, 1925 and June 3, 1926.

Due largely to the collapse of the Florida real estate market, difficulties arose in numerous instances with the buildings under construction, and Miller & Company advanced large sums out of its own funds. On September 25, 1926 the Corporation was adjudicated bankrupt, its assets were insufficient to pay the allowed claims of creditors and the preferred stockholders lost their investment in its entirety. On October 17, 1928 complaints were lodged against the partners of the New York Firm by various groups of the preferred stockholders in the Municipal Court of New York City, in the Supreme Court of New York, and in the United States District Court (alleging that they had relied on the balance sheet, which they asserted had been negligently prepared). The claims of over 1,100 plaintiffs aggregated one million three hundred thousand dollars. In February 1930 the plaintiff's counsel in the District Court cases filed a bill of particulars alleging many errors, but especially in connection with "Notes and Accounts Receivable and Accrued Interest—Secured," "Trust Funds," and "Contingent Liabilities." The pro-forma balance sheet described an asset as "Notes and Accounts Receivable and Accrued Interest—Secured—$2,987,411.69." At the time of the examination, it was honestly believed they were secured. In the trial the jury also believed this. On the "Trust Funds" the pro-forma balance sheet contained the item of "Cash, including time certificates of deposit, $4,663,099.93." Of this $3,000,000 was the cash to be received from the sale of preferred stock, and of the remaining $1,663,099.93 the amount of $1,377,000 represented cash received by G. L. Miller & Company, Inc. from mortgagors for interest, taxes, and bond redemption payments, such cash being held for the bondholders. The plaintiffs claimed that this gave a false impression as to the Company's cash position. The defense was that the liability to the bondholders was set forth on the liability side of the pro-forma balance sheet under a caption "Funds for Bond Interest and Redemption $1,966,938.40" and that this included the $1,377,000 to which reference had been made. In the trial the jury believed that the item on the liability side disclosed the trust obligation. The third point as to disclosure of contingent liabilities was not pressed as were the others.

While these were the chief points, there was the usual exhaustive examination before trial to try to find other possible claims. This ran for weeks and resulted in 1430 pages of testimony.

John R. Wildman took charge of the case, assisted by Edward A. Kracke and Leslie E. Palmer, and they devoted all of their time to preparation of the defense.

Our counsel was Charles P. Rogers of Holmes, Rogers &

Carpenter, who brought in Corbin & Bennett. The trial counsel selected was Governor Nathan L. Miller, who was General Counsel for the United States Steel Company. Saul Levy, (one of the leading authorities on accountants' liability), was also engaged to assist the Firm and followed carefully the preparation of the case and the trial.

The trial in the United States District Court began February 6, 1934, Judge Robert P. Patterson presiding. It lasted seventy court days with detailed examination and cross examination of every phase of the Company's activity and every item in the balance sheet. The accountants on the engagement: E. L. Peed, R. M. Herrick, A. R. Lewis, and K. M. Montgomery testified and were cross examined. Mr. Palmer was a superb witness and spent many days on the witness stand. Mr. Wildman, Mr. Dallas, and Mr. Bell also testified.

Originally the complaint charged Haskins & Sells with negligence in the auditing of the accounts and the certification of the balance sheet. However, in 1931 the Court of Appeals of New York in the case of Ultramares Corp. v. Touche held that an accounting firm could not be held liable to the public for negligence alone, and the complaint against Haskins & Sells was amended to allege willful and knowing fraud on the part of Haskins & Sells in the preparation of the financial statements. The defense contended that the pro-forma financial statements which they certified were honest and accurate reflections of books of G. L. Miller & Company, Inc. after giving effect to the proposed financing and argued that even if inaccuracies should be proven, the statements represented honest judgment of the accountants as to the earnings and financial condition.

As expert witnesses the Firm called John T. Madden, Dean of the New York University School of Commerce, and Dr. Joseph J. Klein, former President of the New York State Society of Certified Public Accountants, and the plaintiffs used Professor William Morse Cole, formerly Professor of Accounting at Harvard University.

There were seven thousand pages of testimony, and six hundred exhibits were received in evidence.

On May 7, 1934 the jury rendered a verdict for the Firm.

The plaintiffs filed an appeal in which elaborate briefs were submitted. It was argued before Judge Swan of the Circuit Court of Appeals January 20, 1937. He rendered a lengthy opinion affirming the judgment in the District Court.

The plaintiffs on December 13, 1937 petitioned the Supreme Court of the United States for a writ of certiorari, which was denied.

The case in the District Court (O'Connor v. Ludlam) had been the test case, but in May 1942 the counsel for the plaintiffs threatened to take up again the case in the New York Supreme Court and the Municipal Court of New York City, hinting for a settlement without trial. After a long meeting with our counsel, Harold H. Corbin, and our trial counsel, Governor Nathan L. Miller, counsel for the plaintiffs decided not to proceed. On September 24, 1942 a stipulation was filed that these actions be settled and discontinued without costs to either party. So after fourteen trying years, the case was finally closed.

This case was one of the first suits against accountants, and one of the very few which were contested successfully by accountants through all of the Courts.

The clear forceful grasp of accounting matters which Judge Patterson displayed was one of the chief reasons for selecting him years later as our counsel in the Thomascolor situation.

A sad note was that the strain of preparing for the trial broke Mr. Wildman's health and he was obliged in 1932 to take almost a year's stay in hospitals and a rest home. It was at this time that the Haskins & Sells Bulletins were discontinued. The death of his wife in October 1932 added to his general depression. He returned in time to testify in the trial, but without his usual vigor. He did not regain full health and died September 21, 1938.

9

Federal Reserve Board Pamphlets—
American Institute of Accountants Special Committee on Uniform Standards of Corporation Accounting and Disclosure—
New York Stock Exchange Action—
Hearings before United States Senate Committee on Banking and Currency—Colonel Carter's Testimony
Securities Act of 1933—Securities Exchange Act of 1934—
Other Federal Legislation—"A Statement of Accounting Principles"—American Institute of Accountants Committees on Accounting and Auditing Procedure

The Federal Reserve Board in 1918 issued a bulletin under the title of "Approved Methods for the Preparation of Balance Sheet Statements." This was revised by the Board in 1929 with a bulletin "Verification of Financial Statements." The Stock Exchange panic later that year and the depression of 1929-1932 brought about national discussion of financial statements of corporations.

In 1930 a Special Committee of the American Institute of Accountants of which Colonel Carter was a member was formed to deal with uniform standards of corporation accounting and disclosure.

In a formal communication addressed September 22, 1932 to the Committee on Stock List the Institute Committee on Cooperation with Stock Exchanges expressed its belief that in the "development of the activities of the Exchange in relation to annual reports of corporations . . . there are two major tasks to be accomplished—one is to educate the public in regard to the significance of accounts, their value and their unavoidable limitations, and the other is to make the accounts published by corporations more informative and authoritative." There followed a dozen pages of exposition of technical subjects germane to the accomplishment of these broad ends and an outline of practical means of continuing cooperation among the Exchange, the Institute, and listed corporations whereby the areas of agreement on disputed principles of accounting might be enlarged and greater uniformity in practices of disclosure attained.

In the resulting correspondence and the measures that were taken substantial progress was made on these matters—not the least of which was the rule adopted by the Exchange in 1933 requiring that financial statements in reports to stockholders be certified by independent auditors. Also, on the subject of form and content of auditors' certificates, agreement was reached on desirable standard clauses which would define the scope of the examination and express the auditor's opinion of the acceptability and consistency of the accounting principles followed by the corporation and the fairness of its presentation of its financial position and results of operations.

On January 6, 1933 the New York Stock Exchange issued a statement requiring independent audits of the accounts of all corporations applying for listing after July 1, 1933 and providing that the scope of the audit must not be less than indicated in the pamphlet entitled "Verification of Financial Statements" issued by the Federal Reserve Board in May 1929.

Congress had before it a bill imposing severe restrictions on the issuance of securities and the Institute Committee's letter of September 22, 1932 was introduced in evidence by the Chairman of the Committee on Stock List at a hearing before the United States Senate Committee on Banking and Currency on January 12, 1933.

Colonel Carter, as President of the New York State Society of Certified Public Accountants, was requested by Senator Fletcher of the Committee on Banking and Currency to express his views regarding the proposed Federal Securities Act. This Colonel Carter did on April 1, 1933 in a carefully prepared statement, which received wide and favorable publicity throughout the Country.

Colonel Carter was the only accountant who appeared to testify during the hearings. His testimony required 12 pages in the printed hearings before the Committee. In this he proposed that the financial statements to be included in a registration statement should be examined by an independent public accountant who should express his opinion with respect to the statements. The legislative history of the Act clearly indicates that the Congress accepted the idea that public accountants by making independent examinations could render a public service in protecting the investor and revised the legislation accordingly.

The exchange of questions and answers before the Senate Committee is interesting:

Mr. Carter. At the end of subsection 4-A of section 5 on page 8 I would suggest that the following be added after the words "actual business":

> "The accounts pertaining to such balance sheet, statement of income and surplus shall have been examined by an independent accountant and his report shall present his certificate wherein he shall express his opinion as to the correctness of the assets, liabilities, reserves, capital and surplus as of the balance sheet date and also the income statement for the period indicated."

That is, three years.

Senator Barkley. How much more and additional employment would that give to certified accountants?

Mr. Carter. Eighty-five per cent of the companies that are listed on the exchanges in New York today are examined.

Senator Reynolds. Do you think it proper to insert in there that these independent public accountants should be privileged to state their opinion as to the value of securities or the condition of the company?

Mr. Carter. We are unable to express an opinion as to the value of securities. I think the impression generally prevails that one who reads a balance sheet and an income statement regards the figures in such a statement as a defensible definitely ascertainable fact, whereas, as a matter of fact in reality it can only be an opinion based upon certain accounting assumptions which must be applied to the opinion of some individual as to values...

Senator Barkley. In other words, after the statement has been filed by the officers of the company you want an independent organization to go over it and then report to the Federal Trade Commission whether that is correct or not?

Mr. Carter. I mean that the statement itself should have been the subject of an examination and audit by an independent accountant.

Senator Gore. Before filing.

Mr. Carter. Before filing.

Senator Gore. Is that patterned after the English system?

Mr. Carter. Yes, sir.

Senator Reynolds. Together with an opinion?

Mr. Carter. That is all they can give. That is all anyone can give as to a balance sheet.

Senator Wagner. Well, basically, are not these facts that have got to be alleged rather than an opinion?

Mr. Carter. Under the terms of the bill it has to be given under oath. I do not see that anyone can certify under oath that a balance sheet giving many millions of dollars of assets is as a matter of fact correct. He can state his opinion based upon a thorough investigation.

Senator Barkley. In other words, before the officers of the company that is issuing stock shall file that statement that is contained in this bill with the Federal Trade Commission the company must call in outside independent accountants and give them the job of going over it and passing on whether they told the truth or not. Well, I am not for your amendment, I will say that now. . . .

Mr. Carter. . . . But there is in the bill a provision which gives the Commission a right to demand such an investigation and demand such a report as a result of such investigation. My point is to put that in the application in the beginning.

Senator Barkley. Do you not think it is more in the interest of the public that is to buy these securities, if there is to be any checkup or any guarantee as to the correctness, that it be done by some government agency rather than by some private association of accountants?

Mr. Carter. I think it is an impractical thing for the government agency to do it effectively.

Senator Reynolds. Why?

Mr. Carter. Because it involves such a large force. It involves the question of time.

Senator Reynolds. Well, it would not require any more time on the part of the government officials to make a checkup and audit than it would by private individuals, would it?

Mr. Carter. I think the public accountant is better equipped to do that than the average government agency would be able to do that...

Senator Barkley. Is there any relationship between your organization with 2,000 members and the organization of controllers, represented here yesterday with 2,000 members?

Mr. Carter. None at all. We audit the controllers.

Senator Barkley. You audit the controllers?

Mr. Carter. Yes; the public accountant audits the controller's account.

Senator Barkley. Who audits you?

Mr. Carter. Our conscience.
Senator Barkley. I am wondering whether after all a controller is not for all practical purposes the same as an auditor, and must he not know something about auditing.
Mr. Carter. He is in the employ of the company. He is subject to the order of his superiors.
Senator Barkley. I understand. But he has got to know something about auditing?
Mr. Carter. Yes.
Senator Barkley. He has got to know something about bookkeeping?
Mr. Carter. But he is not independent. . . .
Senator Reynolds. Why should your members ask that they be permitted and empowered to check these accounts?
Mr. Carter. Because it is generally regarded that an independent audit of any business is a good thing.
Senator Reynolds. All right. Then, after it goes to the Commission they have to check up to see who is right; they have to go through and audit again. There has to be a government audit, as suggested by Senator Barkley. Would it not be creating more difficulty and more expense and more time for the government if auditing organizations interest themselves in these various and sundry corporations? . . . Could they do it more economically than the government?
Mr. Carter. I think so.
Senator Gore. There would not be any doubt about that.
Senator Reynolds. Why?
Mr. Carter. We know the conditions of the accounts; we know the ramifications of the business; we know the pitfalls of the accounting structure that the company maintains. You have got every kind of business to deal with.
Senator Reynolds. Suppose that we decide in the final passage of this bill here to employ five or six hundred auditors from your organization, that would be all right, then, would it not?
Mr. Carter. I do not think the government could employ five or six hundred independent accountants.
Senator Reynolds. Why could they not?
Mr. Carter. I do not think the type of men that are in the public practice of accountancy would leave their present practice to go

in the government employ....

Senator Adams. How much of a burden is this going to put on the comparatively small company? You were speaking a while back of the companies whose stocks are listed being independently audited. Now coming under the control of this bill are going to be thousands of small companies putting out an issue for their original financing. How much of a burden and cost is that going to put on them?

Mr. Carter. Very little measured in value to the investor and to them.

Senator Gore. What would be the range?

Mr. Carter. My experience would be that the average company pays around $500 or $600 or $700 for its auditing, that is, taking the large and small together....And the largest organizations of our country do it and have been doing it for the last 15 years.

Senator Gore. Have had these independent audits made?

Mr. Carter. Have had these independent audits made, yes.

Senator Gore. But they have not been available for any public authority to examine and afford no safeguards?

Mr. Carter. They have been published in their annual reports and distributed to all of their stockholders, to the newspapers and anyone who calls for them.

Senator Gore. And have not done any good?

Mr. Carter. Yes, sir; I think they have.

Senator Gore. We have had all this debacle here in spite of that....

Mr. Carter. Eighty-five per cent of all the companies listed on the New York Stock Exchange have independent audits...

The Chairman. This bill covers all of them, those listed and those not listed.

Mr. Carter. Those are the ones that should be independently audited.

Senator Reynolds. Which ones?

Mr. Carter. Those that are not listed.

Senator Reynolds. All right; the ones that are not listed are the litttle fellows, are they not?

Mr. Carter. Yes, sir.

Senator Reynolds. Could they pay you $75 a day to go into their books?

Mr. Carter. It does not cost them $75 a day.

Senator Reynolds. How much do you charge a day, then?
Mr. Carter. It would cost them an average of, I should say $25 a day.
Senator Kean. What big companies charge $25?
Mr. Carter. That is about an average.
Senator Kean. Marwick, Mitchell & Co. cost more than that.
Mr. Carter. I am giving you an average.
Senator Kean. Waterhouse & Co. cost more than that. What companies do you know of that charge only $25 a day?
Mr. Carter. I said that was an average for all. The rates range from $100 a day for a partner down to $15 and $20 a day for a junior. The average scale of rates that are charged are $35, $30, $25, $20, and $15, depending upon the class of men...
Senator Gore. Don't you think we have got to establish some sort of standard of bookkeeping for different lines of industry before we can make any comparison?
Mr. Carter. I think it is very hard to establish a standard of bookkeeping. You can rely upon principles of accounting....
Senator Gore. I mean the bookkeeping would be standard there so that you could compare one with another, and if they are not standardized give this Commission the power to require them to conform to it?
Mr. Carter. Take the automobile industry. You could have the reports of the various companies and you could find a great similarity in their bookkeeping.
Senator Gore. I know, but unless there is a substantial similarity I do not see how any comparison could be made. You take the textile companies: I presume they may have standards now that they all conform to, but if they do not, don't you think it would be necessary?
Mr. Carter. I think you would have to take each industry itself and... provide a system in which they would set up their accounts peculiar to that particular industry.
Senator Gore. That is what I mean, some sort of standard or set of principles so that each industry and individual instances in each industry could be compared with each other.... Is this mandatory in England, the requirement that an independent accountant shall check up?
Mr. Carter. All companies in England are required to be audited

> by an independent accountant, who is present at the stockholders' meeting and is available to answer any questions the stockholders wish to put to him....

The Securities and Exchange Commission was created by the Securities Exchange Act of 1934, to administer provisions of that law and those of the Securities Act of 1933, which was initially administered by the Federal Trade Commission. Among the extensive regulatory powers conferred upon it were those relating to standards of accounting and financial disclosure of all corporations making public offerings of securities in interstate commerce and through the mails and of all corporations listed and registered upon national securities exchanges. These Acts require that financial statements included in registration statements and periodic reports filed with the Commission be certified by independent public accountants; and the Commission set up rigid criteria of independence.

The Federal regulatory legislation which emerged in the thirties included the Glass-Steagall Banking Act of June 1933, providing, in part, for the separation of commercial and investment banking, and for restrictions on the use of bank credit for speculative purposes. It further included the Public Utility Holding Company Act of 1935, which prescribed certain standards for regulating financial activities and intercompany transactions; it also required simplification of corporate structures and limitation of system operations to geographical integrated units, with consequent divestment of non-related properties. The administration of this Act was placed under the Securities and Exchange Commission, as was that of the Investment Company Act of 1940. The latter required, among other things, the registration of corporations engaged primarily in investing and trading in securities and disclosure of their finances and investment policies; it also prohibited changes in policies without stockholder approval.

These developments in Federal legislation obviously represented, if not a shattering blow to the independence of the public accounting profession, at least a potential danger of the first magnitude. The profession might "all too easily find itself" (said A. A. Berle, Jr.) "merely the ciphering agency for virtually unreviewable bureaucrats." Today, after many years of trial, in the earlier part of which considerable rough ground had to be traversed, the realization of any threat of such proportions seems unlikely. The profession is moving steadily forward to a position where the views of individual members and the progressively better harmonized pronouncements of the Institute on subjects within our field will be accorded respectful attention by directly interested parties, and by disinterested students of affairs.

In the Institute Special Committee's letter of September 22, 1932, to the New York Stock Exchange, one of the principal objects to be striven for was defined as "universal... acceptance by listed corporations of certain broad principles of accounting which have won fairly general acceptance... and within the limits of such broad principles to make no attempt to restrict the right of corporations to select detailed methods of accounting deemed by them to be best adapted to the requirements of their business...." The achievement of this purpose in a sufficiently comprehensive manner was recognized as a task requiring reconcilement of many conflicting views, if agreement, even within the profession itself, was to be extended beyond a small group of broad generalities to comprehend an adequate set of working standards. It was with this need in mind that a committee of three distinguished educators was formed in July 1935 at the invitation of the Haskins & Sells Foundation—a non-profit corporation created in 1928 by five of our senior partners for the purpose, among others, of the "promotion of education and study of useful sciences and especially...accountancy."

The Committee consisted of Thomas H. Sanders (Chairman), Professor of Accounting at the Harvard Graduate School of Business Administration, Henry Rand Hatfield, Professor of Accounting at the University of California, and Underhill Moore, Professor of Law at Yale University. They were asked by the Foundation to make and report upon an independent and impartial study of the subject of accounting principles, and the hope was expressed that there might thus be established "a body of principles which will become useful in unifying thought and which by its acceptance will serve to standardize accounting practices."

The Foundation's invitation further said: "The need for the kind of study suggested has become increasingly apparent, particularly during the past three years. Sharp variations among the statutes of the different jurisdictions have existed for some time. These statutes collectively are not only inconsistent and contradictory, but in some instances they permit practices which are difficult to reconcile with dutiful business management. Federal agencies have issued regulations involving accounting principles which have resulted in contradiction between agencies, and Federal regulations involving such matters conflict frequently with those of state regulatory bodies. The stock exchanges in their efforts to promote greater publicity of corporate financial information, the Federal Government in its administration of the Securities Act of 1933, as amended, designed to afford adequate disclosure with respect to new issues of securities, and through the Securities Exchange Act to insure the same information to the holders of and prospective investors in listed securities, have raised sharply the question as to what are accepted principles of accounting. Notwithstanding the difficulties involved, accountants who certify to financial statements filed with the Securities and Exchange Commission have been required by the regulations of that Commission to express an opinion concerning such financial statements and the practices of the registrant in the light of accepted principles of accounting."

The Committee began its work in the summer of 1935 and completed it two years later with the preparation of the now widely known report, A Statement of Accounting Principles—a text of 116 pages, plus 22 pages of notes of references to legal provisions of concern to accountants. Several thousand copies of this notable volume were distributed to all members of the American Institute of Accountants and numerous other interested persons by the Executive Committee of the Institute as "a highly valuable contribution to the discussion of accounting principles." The American Accounting Association reprinted the Statement in 1959.

In its preface the Committee disclosed in some detail the several lines of inquiry and research which it had pursued. It was clearly a broad-based and logical approach, new to the field of accountancy literature and uniquely valuable to the profession. Coupled with the merits of their research method, the acknowledged competence and impartiality of the Committee members gave to A Statement of Accounting Principles a persuasiveness and weight never previously enjoyed by any pronouncement of comprehensive scope in the annals of accountancy. The book has been widely quoted by courts and commissions and by writers on accounting subjects generally. Without doubt judicial and other governmental authorities, as well as bankers, other business executives, and investors, derived from it a better understanding of the unwisdom of trying to oversimplify some of the inherent complexities of accounting. To many such persons the report made it clearer than before that accounting is far from being an exact science. This thought was presented with sufficient corroborative detail to shed a strong light on a truth which more often than not had eluded the layman; that beyond certain points, often not clearly definable in advance, it becomes impossible to hammer accounting principles into the rigid mold that code-making ordinarily implies; and when, in practice, circumstances indicate to the experienced accountant that such a point has been reached, the exercise of his best judgment—though fallible like any other human judgment—inescapably becomes the final reliance of the layman, so far as past operating results and present financial condition can reasonably be expected to guide the investor in the future employment of his funds.

The American Accounting Association also made a valuable contribution to advanced thinking on a number of subjects by the issuance in 1936 of a Tentative Statement of Accounting Principles.

The American Institute of Accountants in 1939 undertook to enlist the whole profession in assuming a still larger responsibility for the development of sound accounting principles. It set up a Research Department in its office in New York, which was headed successively by Professor Sanders and Professor James L. Dohr on a part-time basis, and by Carman G. Blough, formerly chief accountant of the Securities and Exchange Commission, on a full-time basis. This Department performed notable service, largely in supplementing the work of the technical committees.

The work of the Institute Committee on Accounting Procedure assumed an enhanced internal importance and public position, when it began the publication of a continuing series of Accounting Research Bulletins with an initial Statement in September 1939 setting out their intended purposes and applicability. Under its rules any opinion expressed by the Committee required for its adoption the assent of two-thirds of its twenty-two members; and dissenting members had the right to have their views incorporated in the text of the relevant pronouncement. Further, under its rules: "Recommendations of the Committee are not intended to be retroactive, nor applicable to immaterial items" and "it is recognized that any general rules may be subject to exception: it is felt, however, that the burden of justifying departure from accepted procedures must be assumed by those who adopt other treatment." This Committee started in 1930 and had on it at various times John R. Wildman, William H. Bell, Arthur H. Carter, Arthur B. Foye, John W. Queenan, and Weldon Powell. It was succeeded in 1959 by the Accounting Principles Board.

Events in the late thirties concerned with auditing procedures and particularly their accepted scope, led to the establishment in the Institute of a Committee on Auditing Procedure on a recommendation "that certain additional procedures regarding inventories and accounts receivable should be considered as generally accepted practice" and "that, where these additional procedures ... had not been undertaken, that fact should be disclosed in the auditors' report or opinion." These procedures had been adopted by Haskins & Sells in the middle 1920s.

The report of the Committee on this subject, which was approved by the Council of the Institute in May 1939 and given wide distribution at the time, received widespread approval by interested parties, the press, and the public generally. This report with certain clarifying modifications was approved by the membership of the Institute at the annual meeting in September 1939, and was issued by the Committee as the first of a series of Statements on Auditing Procedures, still periodically promulgated under a constantly widening program of research. The Committee's Statements "represent the considered opinion of the members of the Committee on Auditing Procedure expressed by formal vote after examination of the subject matter by the Committee and the Research Department. Statements of the Committee are not intended to be retroactive nor applicable to immaterial items, and except in cases in which formal adoption by the Institute membership has been secured, the authority of the Statements rests upon the general acceptability of opinions so reached."

Edward A. Kracke was a member of the Committee on Auditing Procedure on its establishment in 1939, and remained on the Committee until his place was taken by Gordon Hill in 1947. Mr. Hill continued on the Committee until 1954 (serving three years as Chairman), and was succeeded by Malcolm M. Devore and later by Oscar S. Gellein and Kenneth Stringer.

In the foregoing there have been outlined some of the more notable developments which reflected a steadily increasing sense of responsibility by the profession. Together with many important public and private contributions by individuals they explain, in part, the high place of technical and moral authority which the public accounting profession has attained.

10

*Colonel Carter becomes Managing Partner—
Important Public Engagements 1931-1937—World War II—
General Carter's Service as Fiscal Director, Army Service Forces—
Colonel Andrew Stewart—Commander George P. Auld—
Arthur B. Foye becomes Managing Partner*

In 1928 and 1929 Mr. Ludlam's failing health kept him in Florida most of the year and in 1930, when Mr. Ludlam retired, Colonel Carter became the Managing Partner.

In January 1931 the Firm took an engagement from the State of Tennessee to make an audit of all State departments and all institutions under such departments, with a survey of the accounting systems and recommendations for improvement therein. The public and the press throughout the State were demanding a thorough investigation, because the State would probably lose several million dollars of State funds deposited in banks or controlled by Caldwell & Co. which failed in the fall of 1930. A joint committee of twelve members of the Senate and House of Representatives was appointed to make the investigation, and this committee engaged Haskins & Sells. The engagement was carried out in March and April 1931 with fifty men under the direction of the partner in charge of the St. Louis Office, J. Harvey O'Connell. It resulted in a comprehensive and helpful report.

In February 1932 an engagement was taken from Secretary Hyde of the Federal Department of Agriculture to review the handling of installment loans to farmers. A system was devised and installed to the complete satisfaction of the Department. This engagement was under the supervision of Edward A. Kracke, and in the course of it he established good relations with many of the influential members of the House and Senate.

Another important Federal engagement came in April 1933, this one from the Reconstruction Finance Corporation to make an examination of the Corporation for the period from February 2 to December

31, 1932. This engagement was completed to the satisfaction of the Corporation and ourselves, and the Firm was later reengaged for the years ended December 31, 1935, 1936 and 1937.

Prior to the Second World War, four more offices were opened: Milwaukee in 1932, Houston in 1937, Louisville in 1939, and Dayton in 1941.

The years 1941 to 1945 were the years of World War II as they involved the United States. The War began in Europe September 1, 1939. American aid to Britain came in 1940. In September of that year the United States agreed to lease 50 over-age destroyers to Great Britain. On May 27, 1941 President Roosevelt declared an unlimited national emergency for the United States, and in August 1941 President Roosevelt and Prime Minister Churchill drafted the "Atlantic Pact." On December 7, 1941 came Pearl Harbor and the declaration of war with Japan and Germany.

In 1940 President Roosevelt had felt the need of strengthening the organization of the Government and he appointed Henry L. Stimson as Secretary of War and Robert P. Patterson as Assistant Secretary of War. They asked Colonel Carter to come to Washington as Executive Accountant in the office of the Under Secretary of War, which he did as of March 26, 1941. This was the beginning of a period of continuous service lasting to December 1945, in which Colonel Carter assumed additional responsibilities from time to time, becoming Fiscal Director, Army Service Forces in May 1943. Appointed Brigadier General in October 1941, he became a Major General in May 1943.

On March 31, 1941, Andrew Stewart joined General Carter in Washington as his first assistant and remained in that capacity until October 1945. He was commissioned a Lieutenant Colonel in March 1942, was promoted to Colonel in September 1942, and was Deputy Director, Office of the Fiscal Director, until his transfer to inactive status in October 1945.

As Fiscal Director, Army Service Forces, General Carter's responsibilities included all disbursing, including payments of allotments and family allowances; accounting; auditing; payroll deductions; distribution of bonds; guaranteed loans and advance payments to contractors; training programs for all fiscal duties including termination of contracts; and establishment of accounting procedures for all lend-lease transactions.

The Fiscal Director took over the handling of all the accounts of

Andrew Stewart, a colonel in World War II, was General Carter's deputy in Washington and later headed an H&S staff of fourteen in an engagement in Japan for General MacArthur's headquarters.

the War Department, decentralizing the activities into four regional offices with a central office in Washington. Accounting procedures were prescribed for all components and the practice was initiated of setting up all liabilities as incurred. Throughout a period of expenditures of unprecedented magnitude, the accounts of the War Department showing obligations and expenditures for each month were completed and circulated in the Fiscal Report not later than the 20th of the following month. Auditing manuals were prepared setting forth procedures for auditing cost-plus-fixed-fee construction and supply contracts, in which the principle of selective auditing was first enunciated for application to Government contracts. Close cooperation was established with the Comptroller General, who, under the law, was required to pass upon the legality of all expenditures, and it was arranged that he would make his examinations at the projects where the necessary information was available instead of in Washington, where all vouchers had previously been sent. These changes resulted in substantial savings in the cost of administration.

Payments of family allowances and allotments were made by the Office of Dependency Benefits with a staff of approximately 10,000 employees, necessitating the issuance of approximately 8,000,000 checks monthly, amounting to about $500,000,000 monthly at the peak; the Army War Bond Office handled pay deductions for the purchase of war bonds and issued approximately $50,000,000 a month; life insurance pay deductions involved premiums of $55,000,000 a month; soldiers' deposit accounts reached a maximum of $240,000,000 with over 700,000 accounts; military personnel overseas were permitted to transmit funds to the United States through disbursing officers and such transfers ran to $84,000,000 in one month.

Training programs were carried on at Duke University and at Fort Benjamin Harrison for both military and civilian personnel covering all phases of fiscal activities in the War Department. Accounting procedures were established for all lend-lease transactions and the fiscal offices in foreign theatres participated in the accounting therefor. The Office of the Fiscal Director headed a mission to North Africa, Italy, and Great Britain to deal with accounting for military government.

General Carter was awarded an Oak Leaf Cluster (in lieu of a second Distinguished Service Medal, the first having been awarded during World War I); Colonel Stewart was awarded the Legion of Merit.

George P. Auld served the United States Navy with distinction in two World Wars and served the cause of peace as assistant to Owen D. Young in the Dawes Plan. He wrote extensively on the economic and financial problems of Europe.

General Carter had been active (as a Colonel) in the military service in World War I. George P. Auld had also been active in that War, as an officer, latterly Commander, in the Navy. He had served in the Supply Corps for many years and from 1915 to 1918 was chief accounting officer in the Navy. In the latter year he went to London as an aide to Admiral Sims; in 1919 he was an assistant financial adviser to the American Peace Mission in Paris; and from 1920 to 1924 was Accountant General of the Inter-Allied Reparations Commission and assistant to Owen D. Young in starting the operation of the Dawes Plan. With this wide and deep experience with postwar Europe, Mr. Auld wrote extensively on its economic and financial problems.

In February 1941 Mr. Auld was invited by Secretary (then Under Secretary) of the Navy James Forrestal to establish a service of inspection of Navy Department procedures in auditing contract costs under the defense procurement programs. Appointed Chief of the Cost and Audit Branch in the Office of the Under Secretary, he organized, throughout the Country, field panels of Navy Supervising Auditors, embracing members of seventy firms of Certified Public Accountants, to conduct periodic inspections of auditing procedures and reviews of contractors' methods of internal control and cost determination. He also served as member of the Navy Price Adjustment Board until resigning from his Navy work for reasons of health in September 1942. Mr. Auld was awarded the Navy Cross (1919) and made an Officer of the French Legion of Honor (1924). He received a letter of appreciation from the Secretary of the Navy (1942).

The War period was of course a difficult one for Haskins & Sells, 408 men going into the service.

The problems of clients were multiplied by war conditions, by new laws and regulations, restrictions of materials, shortage of manpower yet need for greater production and many other complications. The need for accounting services expanded rapidly and greatly so that with the shortage of accountants the War period was one of intense activity and hard work.

General Carter was relieved from Active duty February 8, 1946, returning to Haskins & Sells in April of that year. He completed three years of retirement May 31, 1947 and Mr. Foye, who had been acting managing partner from 1941 to 1946, then became Managing Partner.

11

Postwar Activities and Problems—Thomascolor Incorporated
SCAP Engagement—Service for Commission
on Organization of the Executive Branch of the Government—
Deloitte, Plender, Griffiths & Co.
Merger in the United States—Sir Russell Kettle—
Sir Alan Rae Smith—McLaren, Goode, West & Co. Merger—
Other Mergers 1952-1956—Haskins & Sells "Selected Papers"—
Haskins & Sells Foundation Educational Activities

With the close of the active war in August 1945 there commenced a period of reconversion of industrial facilities to peacetime products, the demobilization of the Armed Forces and their reabsorption into commercial, agricultural, and other fields, the balancing of inventories, and the filling of demands created by wartime shortages. During the War, tremendous strides had been made in the improvement of techniques of production and handling of goods. These adjustments occurred in a period of great economic uncertainty.

The War and the postwar period of adjustment also resulted in new and advanced accounting techniques. During the closing years of the War, the Firm requested its first IBM machines for internal accounting so as to secure early delivery after the War. The era of mechanical equipment had begun.

It was also a time for corporate expansion and development with many old and new corporations registering securities under the Securities Act of 1933. One of these was Thomascolor, Incorporated. In 1947 through one of the prominent New York law firms, Cadwalader, Wickersham & Taft, Haskins & Sells undertook an engagement to examine the accounts of Thomascolor, Incorporated, which was promoting improvement in color photography. The examination was made and financial statements certified. The Securities & Exchange Commission took exception to the filing and the only securities of the registrant sold to the public were 200 shares at $10.00 each. The Securities & Exchange Commission initiated a proceeding against Haskins & Sells in May 1948 and the case was heard and discussed extensively, with 2900 pages of testimony taken. The position of

Haskins & Sells on the highly complicated and extremely difficult technical accounting questions involved was supported by three distinguished accountants of the American Institute of Accountants: Edward B. Wilcox, Samuel J. Broad, and J. S. Seidman. No expert testimony was offered in rebuttal, but the Commission brushed aside the testimony and after two and a half years handed down an order suspending Haskins & Sells for ten days from filing any documents with the Commission.

The decisive issues in this case involved matters of judgment, not only as to the weight and meaning of available accounting evidence, but also the proper accounting treatment to be based thereon. It was felt at the time, even if the Commission were vested with final authority to make an appraisal of the accounting evidence and override the judgment of the accountants who worked on the case and of the three independent experts, this authority should not have been exercised as to conclude that the accountants were involved in professional misconduct because their judgment and conclusions on these technical matters did not coincide with the judgment and conclusions of the Commission.

One of the unusual engagements in this period was the audit for The Supreme Commander for the Allied Powers in Tokyo in 1951 of the foreign exchange funds from September 1947 to March 31, 1951.

At the close of the Second World War, the Potsdam Proclamation issued on July 26, 1945 by the heads of governments of the United States, China, and Great Britain, and subsequently adhered to by the Union of Soviet Socialist Republics, defined the terms for Japanese surrender and stated, as one of the objectives, that Japan should eventually be permitted participation in World trade and access to raw materials.

The directive of the President of the United States to the Supreme Commander for the Allied Powers dated August 13, 1945, authorized him to take the necessary steps to effectuate the surrender terms.

On September 6, 1945 the President of the United States approved the post surrender policy, providing that Japan should be permitted eventually to resume normal trade relations with the rest of the World, but that during the occupation suitable controls would be maintained over all imports and exports of goods and foreign exchange and financial transactions, with the policies followed in the exercise of such controls and their actual administration subject to the approval and supervision of The Supreme Commander.

The H&S staff on the SCAP engagement, Tokyo 1951. From left: Benton Coit, Ronald Scharer, Andrew Stewart, Robert Wagner, John Knepper, Nelson Overbey, John Tillotson, Edward Alberts, Harry Hempy, Leland Wurtz, James Craw, William Phares, Walton Carpenter, Robert Hoffman, Wayne Williamson.

When the Allied Powers occupied Japan, the position of that Country in respect of foreign trade and foreign exchange was briefly:

1 It had no foreign trade.
2 All of its assets of the types ordinarily available for foreign trade and exchange had been either confiscated or become subject to attachment.
3 It had lost most of its former foreign sources of raw material, such as Manchuria, Formosa, China, etc.
4 Its merchant marine had been almost completely destroyed; remaining shipping was taken over by the Occupation Forces and was used for short shipments around Japan.

Under SCAP trade was initiated on a barter arrangement and gradually through a Japanese Board of Trade and the Bank of Japan imports and exports were licensed and controlled, thus starting Japan once more in international trade. From the date of occupation, September 2, 1945, to March 31, 1951, imports and exports aggregated approximately $4,800,000,000. At the latter date the Foreign Exchange Control Board had assets of $522,000,000. We were engaged to make an audit of the foreign exchange funds from September 1947 to March 31, 1951, and to audit the transactions for the period prior to September 1947 to the extent feasible.

This engagement involved a thorough and careful preliminary survey of the background, the organizations involved, and the records available, made in November and December 1950 by one of the partners, J. Wilbur Haines. A group of four principals and ten in-charge accountants from eight offices under a partner, Colonel Andrew Stewart, was assigned to the work in Japan, which took about three months. The comprehensive report was well received.

Another engagement was for The Honorable Herbert Hoover as Chairman of the Commission on Organization of the Executive Branch of the Government and involved financial surveys of Government-owned hydroelectric projects (Boulder Dam—Hoover Dam), fourteen Bureau of Reclamation Projects, the Columbia River Power System (consisting of Bonneville Dam Project—Columbia Basin Project—Grand Coulee Dam—and Bonneville Power Administration), the Southwestern Power Administration, and Tennessee Valley Authority. It also involved financial surveys of

United States Maritime Commission
Rural Electrification Administration

Panama Railroad Company
Federal Prison Industries
Inland Waterways Corporation
Puerto Rican Reconstruction Administration
The Virgin Islands
An extensive report with many recommendations was submitted in August 1948.

As further service to the Government Paul K. Webster, who was made a partner in San Francisco in 1940, and in 1953 became Senior Partner in Los Angeles, resigned temporarily to become Assistant Commissioner of Internal Revenue, where he spent a year in the reorganization of the District offices of the Internal Revenue Service.

The period from 1952 to 1956 was one of expansion through mergers. There were twelve mergers arranged in those years. There had been a group of mergers, twelve in number, in 1919-1923, and then only three between 1923 and 1952, the acquisition of Clarke & Larkin in 1937 in order to practice in Manila, and the acquisition of the practices of George H. Cheyne in Milwaukee in 1932, and Joel Hunter, Jr. in Atlanta in 1942 to bring them into the organization.

Deloitte, Plender, Griffiths & Co., better known as Deloittes, is one of the oldest of the English firms. It was founded in 1845 by William Welch Deloitte—just 50 years before Haskins & Sells. The founder of the Deloitte firm had a prominent position in English accountancy and was a man of force and character. Other partners came into the firm of Deloittes and there evolved the present partnership of Deloitte, Plender, Griffiths & Co. It has a similarity with Haskins & Sells now in that there is no living member in the firm name. William Welch Deloitte died many years ago, and Lord Plender, who was the active head of the firm during the 1920s, died some years ago. In the quality of its personnel and in the quality of its work it ranks with, and perhaps above, the other leading firms of English accountants.

Haskins & Sells had long thought of having closer relations with Deloittes. Colonel Carter and Mr. Morris talked with them in the early 1930s, but it was not feasible at that time to carry out any change in relations. However, in 1951 and 1952 negotiations by Mr. Foye and Mr. Powell with Sir Russell Kettle and Sir Alan Rae Smith resulted in the merger of the United States practice of Deloittes with Haskins & Sells, and the merger of Haskins & Sells in London with Deloittes. Under this arrangement the two senior partners of Deloittes, Sir

Sir Russell Kettle was joint senior partner of Deloitte, Plender, Griffiths & Co. at the merger negotiations with Haskins & Sells in 1952. He was president of the Institute of Chartered Accountants in England and Wales in 1949-50.

Russell Kettle and Sir Alan Rae Smith, became signatories of the general partnership agreement of Haskins & Sells. On their retirement from Deloittes in 1955 and 1956, W. Guy Densem and Robert T. M. McPhail, who became the senior partners of Deloittes, succeeded Sir Russell Kettle and Sir Alan Rae Smith as signatories to the general partnership agreement of Haskins & Sells, but Sir Russell and Sir Alan continued in an advisory capacity in Haskins & Sells until their deaths.

Sir Russell was distinguished especially for his service to the profession, and Sir Alan for his services to the Government.

Sir Russell, who had been for ten years Lord Plender's secretary, became a member of the Deloitte firm on January 1, 1919. In 1929 he accompanied the then Sir William Plender to the Third International Congress of Accountants in New York and met many of the partners of Haskins & Sells.

He was the only accountancy representative on the Companies Act Amendment Committee set up in 1943 by the government and known as the Cohen Committee to formulate suggestions for bringing the law into line with modern requirements as soon as possible after the restoration of peace. The appointment of this committee has been described as a singularly imaginative action and as an example of much foresight on the part of a Government which already had its hands full. Sir Russell received the honour of Knighthood in 1947 in recognition of his work as a member of this committee and for advising the Government on the implementation of the committee's accounting recommendations. He delivered an address at the autumnal meeting of the Institute of Chartered Accountants of England and Wales in 1947 on the accounts and audit provisions of the new act. He served as Chairman of the Accountants Advisory Committee on the Companies Act appointed by the Board of Trade. Sir Russell was a member of The Council of the English Institute and was president of the Institute for 1949-50.

For his Government he served as a member of the Tithe Redemption Commission, as a member of the Joint Stores Committee of the British Red Cross and St. John's War Organization, and as a member of the Railways Arbitration Tribunal established to award compensation for nationalized railways and canals for which the purchase price could not be related to Stock Exchange quotations.

After the merger he came to the Haskins & Sells partners meetings in the United States until ill health in 1960 prevented his traveling.

Lady Kettle accompanied him to the meeting at The Greenbrier in White Sulphur Springs, West Virginia. It was a happy occasion for when he built a modest home in Woking, Surrey, on a corner he reserved of the grounds of his former estate, he called it "Greenbriar" after the West Virginia resort, but characteristically used the English spelling.

While not an etcher himself, he served for many years as treasurer of the Royal Society of Painter-Etchers and Engravers. On his retirement each of ten of the members gave him one of their etchings. Gardening—especially roses—was one of his hobbies. Another was the collection of humorous stories and unusual events, which he put into scrap books and into his conversation. He had a penchant for writing letters to the Times of London and many were published. He read widely, and wrote easily as is evident in his history of the Deloitte firm "Deloitte & Co. 1845-1956."

Alan Rae Smith was on the Deloitte staff prior to the First World War, but left in 1913 to enter the office of a well known firm of merchant bankers. In World War I he served in the Royal Army Service Corps, and in 1916 was seconded to act as chief accountant of the Navy, Army, and Air Force Institutes, where he had to organize all of the accountancy work involved in the growth of the organization from its beginning to a vast trading corporation.

After the War, he returned to Deloittes and was made a partner in February 1919. He had a long record of public service. His appointments by the British Government included membership, and from 1935 to 1940 the chairmanship of the Colonial Development Advisory Committee, for which service he was knighted in 1935.

In 1938 he was appointed by the Imperial War Graves Commission as a member of a special committee to review its expenditures.

During the Second World War, he served as Financial Adviser to the Ministry of Shipping (later the Ministry of Transport) and on numerous affiliated committees dealing with various aspects of shipping and other forms of transport. For these services he was created Knight Commander of the Order of the British Empire in 1948. One of the sad events of the War was the loss of his eldest son, Alan, while a prisoner of the Japanese in Java.

Sir Alan was nominated by the British Government to the Arbitration Tribunal which determined the sum payable to Courtaulds, Ltd. for shares in their important American subsidiary, compulsorily

Sir Alan Rae Smith, K.B.E., joint senior partner in Deloitte, Plender, Griffiths & Co., whose judgment was greatly valued by clients and who was distinguished for his services to Government.

acquired during the War by the British Treasury for sale to American interests.

Among his other Government services, were Financial Adviser in the postwar formation of the National Dock Labour Board and Adviser to the Home Secretary on the revisions of the London taxicab fares in 1950 and 1951, serving as a member of the Taxicab Committee in 1952.

He was deeply interested in international events, and was a member of the Council and honorary treasurer of the Royal Institute of International Affairs from 1943 to his death in 1961.

During his partnership, his ability had been particularly in evidence in the many successful business negotiations he had conducted on behalf of clients. His able and shrewd assessment of practical possibilities in solving difficult problems was well known, and clients greatly valued his judgment on the form and content of their financial statements.

After his retirement, he joined the boards of a few of the Deloitte clients. One of these was the company which owned and operated the Savoy, Berkeley, and Connaught hotels, and when Sir Alan came to the United States to attend the Haskins & Sells firm meetings, he studied thoughtfully and carefully the operation and service of the resort hotels in which the meetings were held so as to make helpful suggestions to the London hotels.

At his home in Westerham (not far from the home of Winston Churchill) the Rae Smiths had an extensive and lovely garden. He had a number of fine old clocks and was meticulous in having them all chime the hours simultaneously. Their home had great charm, perhaps never more evident than on a late fall day when dusk came early and the curtains were drawn across the windows of the snug sitting room with its fine small paintings and Chinese porcelains, sitting in front of the small grate fire with the tea wagon and its gleaming silver nearby, and talking with Sir Alan and Lady Rae Smith about small and large affairs in an atmosphere of friendly warmth.

Another important merger in 1952 was with McLaren, Goode, West & Co.

The firm of McLaren, Goode & Co. was founded by Norman McLaren (the father of N. Loyall McLaren) in 1895 in San Francisco. It was the oldest accounting firm on the Pacific Coast, and Norman McLaren was one of the early Presidents of the California Society

N. Loyall McLaren, a distinguished Californian, became a partner in 1952 when McLaren, Goode, West & Co. merged with Haskins & Sells. He was president of the American Institute of Certified Public Accountants in 1941-42.

of Certified Public Accountants. In 1945 White & Currie of Seattle merged with it, and in 1950 West, Flint & Co. in New York also merged with McLaren, Goode & Co. under the name of McLaren, Goode, West & Co. The firm had offices in San Francisco, Los Angeles, Seattle, and New York with an extensive practice in the United States and abroad.

The merger brought into Haskins & Sells sixteen partners of McLaren, Goode, West & Co., including Norman Loyall McLaren, James A. Runser, Emmett S. Harrington, Lorin H. Wilson, and Michael N. Chetkovich.

Norman Loyall McLaren was born in San Francisco in 1892, and educated at Taft School in Watertown, Connecticut and the University of California (B.A.). He joined his father's firm in 1917. In his activity in professional affairs he was President of the California Society of Certified Public Accountants in 1928, and President of the American Institute of Accountants in 1941-1942 at the outbreak of World War II. In January 1942 he went on active duty as a Commander in the United States Naval Reserve. As Chairman of the New York Division of the Navy Price Adjustment Board he took part in renegotiation of contracts between military suppliers and the Government, retiring as Rear Admiral. Continuing public service he was Treasurer of the United Nations Conference Committee in San Francisco, and later was accounting adviser to the United States Delegation with the Allied Commission on Reparations in Moscow. In 1947 he was a member of a group surveying the Internal Revenue Bureau.

Mr. McLaren has been and is very active in the community life of San Francisco. He was a member of the Executive Committee of the San Francisco Community Chest from 1934-1942, and a member of the California Board of State Harbor Commission in 1945, becoming its President in 1946.

In 1957 he was made a Director of the Federal Reserve Bank of San Francisco. In addition, he has served as Director of many companies, including the Pacific Telephone and Telegraph Company, The Atchison, Topeka and Santa Fe Railway, and The Irvine Company.

His Alma Mater, University of California, honored him in 1961 with the LL.D. degree, and in 1963 the University of San Francisco, of which he is a member of the Board of Regents, conferred a Doctor of Laws degree upon him. He is also a member of the Advisory Board of the Hoover Institution—Stanford University, the Advisory Council of the University of California School of Business Administration, and the President's Council of the California Institute of Technology.

His acquaintance in San Francisco is wide and it extends across the country. Herbert Hoover and Dwight D. Eisenhower were among his close friends. He is one of the few, if not the only one, who have been President of San Francisco's two most distinguished clubs—The Pacific Union Club and the Bohemian Club.

Other mergers between 1952 and 1956 were:

1953	Zimmermann & Company	New York
1954	Stratford, Visse & Company	Portland
1954	Crandall & Reuter	San Diego
1955	Sparrow, Waymouth & Company	San Juan
1955	Rouse, Favret & Company	Cincinnati
1956	Gabrielson, O'Sullivan, Poulson & Co.	Los Angeles
1956	Williams, Clapp & Company	Rochester
1956	Young, Lamberton & Pearson	Honolulu
1956	Irwin-Imig Company	Omaha
1956	Scarborough & Powers	Birmingham

These mergers in contrast with those from 1919-1923 expanded the practice substantially and brought in many effective and able partners, adding much to the strength of the firm.

As a result of a policy of bringing in and promoting principals to partners and the mergers, the number of partners increased from 81 in 1946 to 183 in 1956.

Haskins & Sells has a long tradition of writing and speaking on accounting, economic and world affairs. Charles Waldo Haskins gave many addresses on accountancy, including:

"Accountancy"
"Accountancy: Its Past and Its Present"
"The Progress of Professional Accountancy"
"The Municipal Accounts of Chicago"
"Reform in Municipal Accounting"

and on accounting education, including:

"The Growing Need of the Higher Accountancy"
"The Scope of Banking Education"
"The Place of the Science of Accounts in Collegiate Commercial Education"
"Business Training"

Those on education were from the viewpoint of the Dean of New York

University School of Commerce, Accounts and Finance.

Elijah Watt Sells continued the tradition with papers on accountancy, including:

"The Accounting Profession: Its Demands and Its Future"
"Certified Public Accountancy as a Profession"
"The Natural Business Year"

and on broader fields:

"Corporate Management Compared with Government Control"
"Why Not Lessen the Evils of Present Taxation?" (1922)
"A Plan for International Peace"

Other partners, such as John R. Wildman, William H. Bell, and George P. Auld wrote and spoke extensively as did many other partners.

In 1955 the idea developed that it would be well to record and preserve some of the papers written by Haskins & Sells people, and "Selected Papers" was started for 1955. The foreword stated

> "Upon those entrusted with accounting responsibility rests the obligation to take their place, with their contemporaries, in the forums of accounting discussion. The vitality of accounting springs from the evolution of new concepts and the regeneration of older postulates: it depends upon a capacity to respond to the need for re-examination against changing experience.
>
> The papers reproduced in this volume represent a part of the contributions, during the year 1955 by members of our organization, to discussion of various subjects in fields of interest to accountants."

This volume contained thirty-four papers on a wide variety of subjects, and altogether there have been 630 articles by 252 contributors in the annual volumes of "Selected Papers."

As a sample of the papers the following "Table of Contents" for 1958 shows the scope of the articles.

The Accounting Profession

Opportunities and Challenges Facing the Profession
John W. Queenan
The Arc of the Pacific: 1958-2000
Arthur B. Foye
Some of the More Important Recent Developments in Accounting in the United States
Andrew Stewart
The Accountant's Rôle in Our Rapidly Changing Economy
Harold W. Scott

Rotation of Auditors
N. Loyall McLaren
Rôle and Survival of the Individual Practitioner
Richard H. Grosse
Some Aspects of Accountants' Legal Responsibility
Oscar S. Gellein
Community Service and the CPA
Colin Park
Haskins & Sells Foundation Scholastic Award
Homer E. Sayad
Career Opportunities in Public Accounting
Alexander J. Bitker
What Can Be Done Currently to Improve Educational Preparation for Accounting Practice
Thomas W. Hudson, Jr.

Accounting Principles and Problems

Accounting Principles—Their Nature and Their Origin
Malcolm M. Devore
Accounting Principles and Income-Tax Allocation
Weldon Powell
Allocation of Income Taxes
Ralph S. Johns
Liberalized Depreciation
Homer E. Sayad
Reporting on Cash-Basis Statements
Malcolm M. Devore
Post-Balance-Sheet Events
Robert E. Whyte
Some Accounting Problems in Business Combinations
John S. Schumann

Auditing Procedures and Problems

Auditing Techniques
Presley S. Ford, Jr.
Statistical Sampling Techniques and Their Application to Inventories
Homer E. Sayad
Statement of Auditing Procedure No. 23—Its Importance to Clients
Daniel M. Sheehan
Audit Problems Related to Electronic Data-Processing Installations
James F. Dunn, Jr.

Management Advisory Services

Operations Research
Joseph F. McCloskey
The Field of Management Services as Seen by the CPA
C. Curtis Gabrielson
Setting a Standard for Your Company's Return on Investment
Harvey O. Edson

Recent Developments in Data Processing
PAUL W. PINKERTON
The Use of Electronic Equipment in Business
ROBERT G. WRIGHT
Electronic Data Processing—Programming for the Internal Auditor
VIRGIL F. BLANK
How Computers Are Applied to Accounting Functions
WALTER H. HANSHAW
An Effective Approach to Control Report Problems
GORDON L. MURRAY
Cost Reduction, How and Where to Apply it
ALFRED L. HUNT
Cost Accounting and Computers
MAURICE S. NEWMAN

Tax Considerations

Tax and Financial Considerations Affecting Choice of Inventory Systems
THOMAS J. GRAVES
Gifts Through Private Charitable Organizations
THOMAS W. HUDSON, JR.
Electing Small-Business Corporations—A New Tax Concept
PAUL MESTERN
Collapsible Corporations
BERTRAM E. GILL
Corporate Liquidations
CHARLES N. WHITEHEAD
Stock Redemptions
JACK MACY
Reimbursed Expenses
THOMAS J. GRAVES
Travel and Entertainment Expenses
EDWARD L. POWERS
Deductions Peculiar to Individuals
PRESLEY S. FORD, JR.

In 1956 Haskins & Sells Foundation adopted a long range program for financial assistance to students majoring in accounting and to universities throughout the Country. The Foundation was organized October 26, 1928 under the Membership Corporation law of New York State with the following incorporators: Charles S. Ludlam, Arthur H. Carter, Arthur S. Vaughan, Charles E. Morris, and Arthur B. Foye. The purposes were stated to be:

To make donations to legally constituted charitable, educational, scientific, religious, literary, library, patriotic and historical institutions and associations.

To make donations for benevolent purposes, including the

promotion of education and study of useful sciences and especially in connection with the profession of accountancy.

Assistance of such accountants and employees of accounting firms, who may be incapacitated by age, infirmity or physical disability, and the education and support of their dependent families, as in the judgment of the directors may be deserving.

To promote the well-being of mankind.

The original emphasis was on the third purpose—"assistance of such accountants and employees of accounting firms who may be incapacitated by age, infirmity or physical disability, and the education and support of their dependent families." With this in mind grants of monthly payments were made to a number of retired employees and dependent families. As time went on, it seemed wise for the Firm itself to make provisions for the pensioning of employees and help to their dependent families. The practice of making such grants by the Foundation was gradually discontinued, the Firm taking over the last three in 1970.

Specific educational grants were made prior to 1956, but in that year the plan was adopted of recognizing by an award of $500 to one of the five students majoring in accounting who had the highest scholastic records in accounting subjects at the completion of their junior year, and grants of $1,000 annually for some qualified students who had expressed an interest in a teaching career, but were unable to plan on three to five years of graduate study. This annual grant was later increased to $2,500. Over the years from 1956 to 1968 scholastic awards have been made in one hundred colleges or universities, and thirty grants to prospective teachers in colleges and universities. The scholastic awards have totaled $389,000, and the grants to prospective teachers $398,625. Other important educational grants have been made, including a matching grant for contributions to the Weldon Powell Professorship in Accountancy at the University of Illinois, which matching grant is in excess of $80,000.

The initial contributions to the Foundation were made by the Firm. The Fund was very substantially increased by Charles S. Ludlam, who left his estate in trust for two life tenants with the Foundation as the remainderman. Both life tenants are now deceased. Additional contributions have been made by partners of the Firm. The Foundation principal is now slightly in excess of $2,000,000.

12

John W. Queenan becomes Managing Partner—Accounting Principles Board—Mergers 1957-1970—Commission on a Study of the Common Body of Knowledge of CPAs—General Activity in the American Institute of Certified Public Accountants—Presidents of State Societies

In 1956 John W. Queenan became Managing Partner of the Firm. He was born in Aurora, Illinois January 11, 1906, by coincidence the same month and day as Mr. Haskins. Another coincidence was that Mr. Sells was with the Chicago, Burlington and Quincy Railroad in the 1870s. Mr. Queenan's father was a Division Superintendent in 1922. The railroad is now a client of Haskins & Sells.

Mr. Queenan graduated from the University of Illinois in 1927 and applied for a position with the Chicago Office of Haskins & Sells, but was rejected as being too young. Fortunately, he was engaged for the Executive Office, coming to it July 1, 1927 in the Technical Procedure Department under John R. Wildman. He was transferred to Newark in 1928, and then to Chicago in 1930. In 1931 he passed his examination for Certified Public Accountant in Illinois, being awarded the gold medal of the Illinois Society of CPAs for the highest grade. He returned to Newark in 1934 and became Manager of the office in 1936. He was admitted to the Firm in 1939. Again he went to Chicago in 1940, remaining until he came to the Executive Office on September 16, 1946.

Mr. Queenan, who later became its President, had long taken an active part in the American Institute of Certified Public Accountants, heading a number of important Committees. One of these was that of Cooperation with the Bar.

In the years leading up to 1954, relations between lawyers and CPAs in tax practice had become confused. Claims and counterclaims from both professions had caused friction that threatened to interfere with serving the public. In 1954 Maurice H. Stans, then President of the American Institute of CPAs, who was later to become Budget Director

Haskins & Sells experienced great growth and development under John W. Queenan's leadership as managing partner. He was president of the American Institute of Certified Public Accountants in 1961-62 and member of the Accounting Principles Board.

in President Eisenhower's administration, and Secretary of Commerce in President Nixon's cabinet, asked Mr. Queenan to help set up a National Conference of Lawyers and CPAs.

With William L. Jameson, who was soon named a Federal Judge, and then with Dean Erwin N. Griswold of Harvard Law School, Mr. Queenan worked out an interprofessional agreement in tax practice. Besides setting forth guiding principles, the men traveled widely to mediate specific grievances between lawyers and CPAs.

In 1956, the United States Treasury Department issued a statement that finally resolved the controversy.

Mr. Queenan also served the Institute in its Council and as Vice President. He was elected President in 1961. He continued his work for the Institute as a member of the Accounting Principles Board. In 1968 the Institute awarded him its gold medal for distinguished service to the profession.

In the Illinois Society he served on two committees, chairman of one of them, was a member of the Special Board of Examiners in Accountancy, and a member of the Board of Directors. Active in the New Jersey Society he served on eight committees, and was twice Treasurer of the Society. Mr. Queenan holds certificates in thirty states, two of them by written examination—Illinois and New Jersey.

In 1970 he received the Illini Achievement Award of the University of Illinois Alumni Association.

He also served the New York State Society of Certified Public Accountants as Chairman of Committees, as a member of the Board of Directors, and as Vice President.

During the period of his leadership of the Firm, there was great growth and development, growth in practice, in offices, partners and staff, and in development of professional and technical accomplishments.

The domestic practice was expanded with the following mergers.

1957	W. L. Schnatterly & Company	Seattle
1958	Henderson, Henderson & Dobbins	Hilo
1958	Miller, Franklin, McLeod & Co.	Rochester
1959	Johnson, Millett, Stott & Brooksby	Phoenix
1959	Wells, Baxter & Miller	Salt Lake City
1960	Palmer and Urner	San Diego
1960	Dranguet, Foote & Company	Dallas
1961	Pentland, Purvis, Keller & Co.	Miami
1961	Redeker, Stanley, Ahlberg & Wilch	Denver

1961	Barnes, Askew, Mills & Company	Atlanta
1961	D. Wayne Ashby Jr.	Columbus
1962	Hiram E. Decker & Company	Chicago
1962	Charles S. Rockey & Company	Philadelphia
1963	George K. Watson & Company	Philadelphia
1963	Phillips, Sheffield, Hopson, Lewis & Luther	Houston
1963	Arnold, Hawk & Cuthbertson	Dayton
1964	Robert O. Douglas & Company	Boston
1965	Homer K. Jones & Company	Memphis
1967	W. O. Ligon & Company	Tulsa
1969	Francisco A. Arabia	San Juan
1969	Milledge, Sinclair, Mendel & Co.	Houston
1969	Rutten, Welling & Company	Detroit
1970	Lewis & Montag	San Antonio
1970	Stanley H. Malis & Co.	Hartford
1970	Spark, Mann & Co.	Boston
1970	Weinstein & Timm	New Haven

The practice abroad was expanded and strengthened with new offices of Deloitte, Plender, Haskins & Sells: four in Canada, one in Central America, five in South America, twelve in Europe, and one in Japan.

Mr. Queenan also served his Community of Greenwich, Connecticut for four years as a member of the Board of Estimate, the town government's budgetary unit, and as Chairman of the Special Gifts Committee of the Community Chest. He has also been Treasurer of the Greenwich Country Club. This was in accordance with his policy of encouraging men in the Firm and accountants generally to be active in community affairs. He has pointed out that relatively few people have the chance to appraise a CPA's technical competence. Many people, however, can observe his standards in community affairs and conclude that he applies the same standards in his professional life.

During the period when Mr. Queenan was Managing Partner there were major developments in the American Institute of Certified Public Accountants. The Accounting Principles Board was organized in 1959. Weldon Powell had been Chairman of the Special Committee of the Institute, whose report led to the establishment of the new research program, and he became the first Chairman of the Accounting Principles Board and planned its organization. This Accounting Principles Board was to supervise the basic research necessary to identify and define accounting principles, to consider the practical application of such research, and to recommend the extent of their acceptability to the profession. The predecessor group, the Committee on Accounting Procedure, dealt with comparability in selected circumstances. At various times over 21 years, the Committee on Accounting Procedure considered the need for a comprehensive statement of accounting principles, but did not formulate one.

On its establishment in 1959 the Accounting Principles Board set out to identify the postulates of accounting and the associated broad accounting principles. The first four years of the Board, when its Chairman was Weldon Powell, were given largely over to the formation of a research group, to clarification of purposes and methods of operation, and to consideration of initial studies developed by the new research arm.

The Board has proceeded to develop studies and make pronouncements. Mr. Queenan succeeded Mr. Powell on the Board and in turn was succeeded by Mr. Harrington.

Another contribution to the profession was the Chairmanship by Elmer G. Beamer of a Commission on a "Study of the Common Body of Knowledge of CPAs." This Commission was composed of five CPAs in public practice (Elmer Beamer, Richard S. Claire, Leonard Price, Marvin L. Stone, and Robert M. Trueblood), and three in education (Sidney Davidson, University of Chicago, Charles E. Johnson, University of Oregon, and Robert K. Mautz, University of Illinois), and Courtney Brown, Dean, Graduate School of Business, Columbia University, Milton Drake, Senior Vice President, The Detroit Bank & Trust Company, Henry P. Hoffstot, Jr., Pittsburgh attorney, and Philip West, Vice President, New York Stock Exchange. Two men were engaged to carry out the Study, Robert H. Roy, Dean of Engineering Science at The Johns Hopkins University, and Professor James H. MacNeill, Chairman of the Department of Accounting Instruction in the School of Business Administration of Fordham University.

After a three-year inquiry, jointly financed by the American Institute of Certified Public Accountants and The Carnegie Corporation of New York, the report entitled "Horizons for a Profession" was written and published.

The report deals with what a CPA should know as he sets forth in his career. It suggests a clear understanding of accounting, an appreciation of two social sciences—economics and the behavior of organizations—a good knowledge of business law, facility in mathematics, a knowledge of finance, production and marketing, a code of ethics, not as a collection of rules, but as a set of personal standards and competence in written and spoken English. The report summed it up by saying:

> "The beginning CPA must have a conceptual grasp of accounting, its interdisciplinary aspects, the environment in which it functions, and of those bodies of knowledge which are ancillary to its central purpose. Finally, he must be prepared to grow with changing conditions and ideas."

The Commission did not expect that overnight young men would begin to experience the sort of education the Report envisioned. However, with growing maturity they expected the men to learn

> "When to speak out, when to be silent, how to say or write that which is necessary but awkward, courage to face up to the need for so doing, talent to be firm yet diplomatic, imagination to see beneath and beyond the surface, perception not only for what has happened but also for what may happen, constancy in ethical behavior, sagacity to avoid errors of omission as well as those of commission; these and other attributes, not definable as knowledge . . . without them a CPA can be nothing more than a technician, regardless of the scope of his knowledge; possessing these attributes plus requisite knowledge, he is a professional."

The introductory profile of the educated accountant and the concluding essay on "The Power to Grow" were written by Mr. Beamer. The study will have long and great impact on the profession. Mr. Beamer in 1970 was awarded The American Institute of Certified Public Accountants Gold Medal for distinguished service to the profession.

The record of activity in the affairs of the American Institute of Certified Public Accountants is indicated by the listings for 1967, 1968, and 1969, which follow:

1967

Vice-President
E. C. Leonard, Jr., Tulsa

Members of Council
Elected and Appointed Members
Ralph T. Bartlett, Newark
Elmer G. Beamer, Cleveland
Jerome A. Benning, Minneapolis
Curtis H. Cadenhead, Dallas

Presley S. Ford, Jr., Tulsa
Thomas J. Graves, San Francisco
Thomas B. Hogan, New York
J. William Stewart, Jr., Charlotte
Lawrence M. Walsh, Philadelphia

Past Presidents of AICPA
Arthur B. Foye, Executive Office
N. Loyall McLaren, San Francisco
Jay A. Phillips, Houston
John W. Queenan, Executive Office

Committee Chairmen
Elmer G. Beamer, Cleveland; Education and Experience Requirements for CPAs
Emmett S. Harrington, Executive Office; Practice Review
Ralph S. Johns, Chicago; Professional Ethics
Eugene L. Larkin, Jr., New York; Bank Accounting and Auditing
Homer L. Luther, Houston; Professional Development Board

Committee Members
Jerome A. Benning, Minneapolis; Relations with Federal Power Commission
Charles L. Clapp, Executive Office; International Relations
Lyndon C. Conlon, Miami; Relations with Civil Aeronautics Board
Malcolm M. Devore, Executive Office; Executive (until January 8, 1967)
Arthur B. Foye, Executive Office; Trial Board
William D. Gasser, Rochester; Board of Examiners
Oscar S. Gellein, Executive Office; Auditing Procedure
Thomas J. Graves, San Francisco; Relations with the Bar
Richard H. Grosse, Pittsburgh; Nominations
Walter H. Hanshaw, Chicago; Data Processing
Ralph S. Johns, Chicago; Relations with SEC and Stock Exchanges
Norman R. Kerth, New Orleans; Subcommittee on Determination of Taxable Income
T. Milton Kupfer, Executive Office; Subcommittee on Responsibilities in Tax Practice
Edwin R. Lang, Executive Office; Relations with Universities
Eugene L. Larkin, Jr., New York; Relations with Bankers and Other Credit Executives
E. C. Leonard, Jr., Tulsa; Executive
Gordon L. Murray, Executive Office; Management Services
Robert D. Niemeyer, Chicago; Consulting Editor for *Management Services*
Neil F. O'Connell, New York; Financial Management and Controls
Fred M. Oliver, Salt Lake City; Advisory Committee to the National Committee on Governmental Accounting
John W. Queenan, Executive Office; Accounting Principles Board, APB Fiscal Committee
J. Edward Robertson, Executive Office; Consultant on Relations with Small Business Administration
Philip J. Sandmaier, Jr., Philadelphia; Editorial Advisory Board
John S. Schumann, Executive Office; Accountants' Legal Liability

Russell P. Shomler, Atlanta; Relations with Federal Home Loan Bank Board
Robert F. Skeehan, Chicago; Subcommittee on Taxation of Corporate Distributions and Adjustments
Charles G. Steele, San Francisco; Statistical Sampling
Kenneth W. Stringer, Executive Office; Planning
Carl L. Sturgis, New York; Stock Brokerage Accounting and Auditing
Russell D. Tipton, Newark; Relations with Interstate Commerce Commission, Uniform Bond Indenture
Robert B. Van Arsdale, Washington, D.C.; Delegate to United States Chamber of Commerce
Robert E. Whyte, Los Angeles; National Defense
Karl R. Zimmermann, New York; Relations with Investment Companies

1968

Members of Council

Elected and Appointed Members

Ralph T. Bartlett, Newark
Elmer G. Beamer, Cleveland
Curtis H. Cadenhead, Dallas
Thomas J. Graves, San Francisco
Thomas B. Hogan, New York
Donald L. Krier, Milwaukee
E. C. Leonard, Jr., Tulsa
Warren K. Reed, Baltimore
J. William Stewart, Jr., Charlotte
Lawrence M. Walsh, Philadelphia

Past Presidents of AICPA

Arthur B. Foye, Executive Office
N. Loyall McLaren, San Francisco
Jay A. Phillips, Houston
John W. Queenan, Executive Office

Committee Chairmen

Elmer G. Beamer, Cleveland; Education and Experience Requirements for CPAs
Malcolm M. Devore, Executive Office; Independence
Emmett S. Harrington, Executive Office; Accounting Trends and Techniques
Eugene L. Larkin, Jr., New York; Bank Accounting and Auditing
E. C. Leonard, Jr., Tulsa; By-Laws

Committee Members

Ralph T. Bartlett, Newark; Awards
Jerome A. Benning, Minneapolis; Relations with Federal Power Commission
Robert J. Cisneros, New York; Investment Companies
Charles L. Clapp, Executive Office; International Relations
Benton C. Coit, San Francisco; Atomic Energy Commission
Lyndon C. Conlon, Miami; Relations with Civil Aeronautics Board

John W. Gilbert, Philadelphia; Subcommittee on Determination of Taxable Income
Thomas J. Graves, San Francisco; Relations with the Bar
Walter H. Hanshaw, Houston; Data Processing
Norman R. Kerth, New Orleans; Subcommittee on Special Tax Problems
T. Milton Kupfer, Executive Office; Subcommittee on Responsibilities in Tax Practice
Edwin R. Lang, Executive Office; Relations with Universities
E. C. Leonard, Jr., Tulsa; Executive
William B. Mansfield, Denver; Health Care Institutions
Don A. Nelson, Los Angeles; National Defense
Robert D. Niemeyer, Chicago; Management Services, Consulting Editors for Management Services
Neil F. O'Connell, New York; Financial Management and Controls
Paul W. Pinkerton, New York; Insurance Accounting and Auditing
John W. Queenan, Executive Office; Accounting Principles Board, APB Fiscal Committee
J. Edward Robertson, Executive Office; Relations with Office of Economic Opportunity
Philip J. Sandmaier, Jr., Philadelphia; Ethics, Editorial Advisory Board—Journal of Accountancy
John S. Schumann, New York; Accountants' Legal Liability
Russell P. Shomler, Atlanta; Savings and Loan Accounting and Auditing
Robert F. Skeehan, Chicago; Subcommittee on Taxation of Corporate Distribution and Adjustments
Charles G. Steele, San Francisco; Statistical Sampling
Kenneth W. Stringer, Executive Office; Auditing Procedure
Carl L. Sturgis, New York; Stock Brokerage Accounting and Auditing
Russell D. Tipton, Newark; Relations with Interstate Commerce Commission
Armin C. Tufer, Executive Office; Advisory Panel on Compliance Reporting
Robert B. Van Arsdale, Washington, D.C.; Consultant on Relations with Department of Housing and Urban Development, Delegates to the United States Chamber of Commerce
Robert E. Whyte, Los Angeles; Practice Review
Lorin H. Wilson, Los Angeles; CPA Examination Content Study

1969

Vice President

Elmer G. Beamer, Cleveland

Members of Council

Elected and Appointed Members

Ralph T. Bartlett, Newark
Elmer G. Beamer, Cleveland
Thomas J. Graves, San Francisco
Ernest H. Kenyon, Omaha
Chauncey A. Norton, Detroit

Homer E. Sayad, Saint Louis
James A. Wilson, Newark

Past Presidents of AICPA

Arthur B. Foye, Executive Office
N. Loyall McLaren, San Francisco
Jay A. Phillips, Houston
John W. Queenan, Executive Office

Committee Chairmen

Elmer G. Beamer, Cleveland: By-Laws, Education and Experience Requirements for CPAs
Malcolm M. Devore, Executive Office: Independence
Robert F. Dickey, Chicago: Finance Companies
Oscar S. Gellein, Executive Office: SEC and Stock Exchanges
T. Milton Kupfer, Executive Office: Federal Taxation—Taxation of Special Entities and Industries
Fred M. Oliver, Salt Lake City: Governmental Accounting and Auditing
J. Edward Robertson, Washington: Office of Economic Opportunity
John S. Schumann, New York: Accountants' Legal Liability
Lorin H. Wilson, Los Angeles: Annual Meeting

Committee Members

Ralph T. Bartlett, Newark: Awards
Elmer G. Beamer, Cleveland: Executive
Charles L. Clapp, Executive Office: International Relations
Benton C. Coit, San Francisco: Atomic Energy Commission
Harold L. Coltman, San Francisco: Manufacturing Management
Malcolm M. Devore, Executive Office: Relations with ACME
James A. Gallagher, New York: Bank Accounting and Auditing
John W. Gilbert, Philadelphia: Federal Taxation—Tax Determination
Robert S. Gorab, New York: Data Processing
Emmett S. Harrington, Executive Office: Accounting Principles Board
Thomas B. Hogan, Executive Office: Office of Foreign Direct Investment
Thomas W. Hudson, Jr., Greensboro: Savings and Loan Accounting and Auditing
Ralph S. Johns, Chicago: Trial Board
Richard B. Keigley, New York: Relations with the Bar
John Byrne Kelly, Cleveland: Health, Education and Pension Funds
T. Milton Kupfer, Executive Office: Federal Taxation—Executive Group
Edwin R. Lang, Executive Office: Relations with Universities
E. C. Leonard, Jr. Tulsa: Professional Ethics—Advisory Committee on Promotional Practice, State Societies
Edward J. Lill, New York: Stock Brokerage Accounting and Auditing
William B. Mansfield, Denver: Health Care Institutions
Don A. Nelson, Los Angeles: National Defense
Robert D. Niemeyer, Executive Office: Consulting Editors for Management Services, Management Services

Neil F. O'Connell, New York: Financial Management and Controls
Paul W. Pinkerton, New York: Insurance Accounting and Auditing
John W. Queenan, Executive Office: American Institute Benevolent Fund, Inc.
Haldon G. Robinson, Executive Office: Accounting Trends and Techniques
Philip J. Sandmaier, Jr., Philadelphia: Nominations, Professional Ethics—Advisory Committee on Technical Standards
Homer E. Sayad, St. Louis: Federal Power Commission
Robert F. Skeehan, Chicago: Federal Taxation—Taxation of Corporate Distributions and Adjustments
Jerome P. Solari, San Francisco: Federal Taxation—Nature and Role of CPA in Tax Practice
Charles G. Steele, San Francisco: Statistical Sampling
Kenneth W. Stringer, Executive Office: Auditing Procedure
Russell D. Tipton, Newark: Interstate Commerce Commission
Armin C. Tufer, Executive Office: Advisory Panel on Compliance Reporting
Robert B. Van Arsdale, Washington: Farm Credit Administration, Department of Housing and Urban Development
Harry R. Weyrich, Executive Office: Editorial Advisory Board—*The Journal of Accountancy*
Robert E. Whyte, Los Angeles: Practice Review
Charles W. Wilkins, Kansas City: Civil Aeronautics Board
Lorin H. Wilson, Los Angeles: CPA Examination Content Study

Another evidence of the activity of Haskins & Sells people is the following list of those who have been Presidents of State Societies. There are many others who have been other officers in the State Societies, members of State Boards of Examiners, and officers in the National Association of Accountants and the American Accounting Association. Those who have served on State Societies and American Institute of Certified Public Accountants Committees are legion.

Presidents of State Societies

Alabama	James J. Scarborough
	Edward L. Powers
Arizona	George Wesley Johnson
	Max A. Millett
California	N. Loyall McLaren
	Paul Webster
	Malcolm M. Devore
	C. Curtis Gabrielson
Colorado	T. Raymond Young
	Allen Redeker
	Thomas E. Stanley
	Andrew Fielding
	Fred P. Carleton
	Axel C. Åhlberg
	C. Howard Kast
Florida	Hugh F. Purvis
	James L. Keller, Jr.
	Lyndon C. Conlon
Georgia	Mack H. Barnes, Sr.
	Edwin H. Henderson
Hawaii	Edward Leigh Bliss
	Stanley Rosch
	Henry J. Sebastian
Illinois	William P. Bickett
	George W. Rossetter
	F. B. Andrews
	Robert F. Dickey
Louisiana	Henry J. Jumonville
	George E. Conroy
	Gayle L. Dalferes

Maryland	Raymond C. Reik
	Edward Fuller
	Charles C. Croggon
	Raymond E. North
	J. Elwood Armstrong
	William B. Tittsworth
	J. Edward Robertson
	Warren K. Reed
Massachusetts	Norman H. S. Vincent
	Arthur W. Koelbel
	Norman E. Jones
Michigan	Frederick N. Tilton
	Cyril N. Bullock
	Harold W. Scott
	Arthur W. Koelbel
	Ralph J. Kliber
	Chauncey A. Norton
Minnesota	Archibald F. Wagner
	Otto S. Pelzer
	Emil F. Bohne
	Jerome A. Benning
Missouri	J. Harvey O'Connell
	John F. Neumayer
	Homer E. Sayad
Nebraska	Jacob H. Imig
	Robert W. Johnson
	Joseph T. Sullivan
	Lawrence F. Chandler
	Ernest H. Kenyon
New Jersey	Ralph S. Johns
	Casper B. Apple
	Ralph T. Bartlett
	James A. Wilson
New York	Charles Waldo Haskins
	Howard B. Cook
	Andrew Stewart
	Edward A. Kracke
	Arthur H. Carter
	George Cochrane
	Arthur B. Foye
North Carolina	Orion N. Hutchinson
	Kay J. Jennell
	J. William Stewart, Jr.
Ohio	George R. Lamb
	Harry W. Cuthbertson
	Julian A. Hawk
	Oliver W. Seifert
	Edmund A. Clarke
	Frank L. Arnold
	Elmer G. Beamer
Oklahoma	Virgil S. Tilly
	Vincent M. Kelly
	E. C. Leonard, Jr.
	Presley S. Ford, Jr.
Oregon	Pearce C. Davis
	Ralph B. Stratford
	Harry C. Visse
Pennsylvania	Charles S. Rockey
	Robert Caldwell
	Richard H. Grosse
Puerto Rico	William A. Waymouth
	Fernando J. Domenech
Rhode Island	Howard K. Sullivan
	Lynd E. Cohick
Texas	Jay A. Phillips
	Harry D. Hopson
	Curtis H. Cadenhead
	Homer L. Luther
Utah	Lynn E. Baxter
	Donald A. Miller
	Z. Vernon Derrick
	Fred M. Oliver
	August Glissmeyer, Jr.
Washington	Rodney D. White
	Lorin H. Wilson
Wisconsin	Olin W. Christopherson
	Donald L. Krier

13

International Practice

As mentioned in Chapter 2, Haskins & Sells opened its first international practice office in London in 1901. This was used as a base for serving our American clients in England and on the Continent. William Holding was the Manager from 1910 to 1916, when he was called up "for service in the War." To take his place, Arthur M. Lovibond, who had been with Haskins & Sells from 1907 to 1912, was reemployed and sent to London in June 1916 as Manager. This began a long period of service for him in Europe, which lasted until 1940, when he was in the process of his retirement. Lovibond went to London with a letter of introduction from Mr. Sells to Sir William Plender of Deloitte, Plender, Griffiths & Co.

World War I brought the United States closer to Europe, as it did the Firm. Mr. Sells from 1901 had always had a broad international outlook. At the close of the War, Mr. Ludlam was asked by the United States Government to go to Paris as accountant for the United States Liquidation Commission, which was to liquidate American supplies and to settle the claims between the United States and the Allies growing out of the War. The staff which accompanied him consisted of three Majors, six Captains, sixteen Lieutenants, thirty privates, and the necessary force of secretaries, stenographers and clerks. The work took many months. Colonel Carter, who had been brought into the Firm to help develop our practice, made a number of trips immediately after the War to England and France.

All of this led to the opening of an office in Paris March 15, 1920 briefly under Howard Garner, and then from November 1921 under Arthur Lovibond. To provide more space in London the office there was moved from 30 Coleman Street to 7 Wormwood Street, Old Broad Street—still in the heart of the "City." In the same year of 1920 offices were opened in Havana and Shanghai to serve American clients.

The practice of serving American clients in connection with their manufacturing and distribution centers abroad was expanded by the influx of American capital in Europe, especially in Germany. The collapse of the German financial structure in 1922 and 1923 precipitated a crisis in European affairs. On November 15, 1923 a dollar was worth 2½ billion marks. The Allied Reparations Commission appointed General Charles G. Dawes and Owen D. Young as United States experts to report on means of balancing Germany's budget and stabilizing its currency. Dawes was selected as Chairman and the Committee's report, known as the Dawes plan, was accepted in 1924 by all the powers concerned. The plan made the actual transfer of reparations payments conditional on the stability of the German exchange. Owen D. Young was given the task of installing the Dawes plan, and in this he was assisted by George P. Auld. Mr. Auld had served during the War as Chief Accounting Officer of the United States Navy. In 1919 he was attached to the American Commission to Negotiate Peace as an assistant financial adviser. From 1920 to 1924 he was Accountant General of the Reparations Commission, and in the latter year he assisted Mr. Young in installing the Dawes plan. Mr. Auld joined Haskins & Sells in Paris in March 1924. He believed there was great need for American capital abroad, especially in Germany and was convinced of the safety of American foreign loans.

Some of the American investment bankers had the same belief and became more and more involved in the financing through bonds of European utilities, manufacturing and extractive industries. In 1925 there was to be found in Berlin a representative of practically every bond house in New York. It was in connection with these financings that Mr. Kracke spent some years in Germany, France, and Italy. Immediately following the successful flotation of the $200,000,000 German external loan in 1924 an office was opened in Berlin and substantial practice developed there.

Colonel Carter in his trips to London developed Mr. Sells acquaintance with Sir William Plender and the other senior partners in Deloitte, Plender, Griffiths & Co., Percival D. Griffiths, Lionel Maltbie, and Arthur E. Cutforth. He and Charles E. Morris talked with them as to closer relations in North America and as a result an agreement was entered into October 1, 1924 for the formation of Deloitte, Plender, Haskins & Sells to conduct under its name the practices of Deloittes and Haskins & Sells in Canada, Cuba, and Mexico—with offices in Montreal, Havana, and Mexico City. This was followed in the late 1920s and early 1930s by the formation of Deloitte, Plender, Haskins & Sells firms in Argentina, Uruguay, Brazil, Chile, Bolivia, Peru, and the Union of South Africa. All of these D.P.H. & S. offices proved to be technically competent and administratively efficient. It has been necessary to close only one office, namely Havana, closed in the early 1960s because of the policies of the Castro regime in Cuba.

Haskins & Sells had good relations with Van Dien, Van Uden & Co. going back to 1905, when an announcement was made in English and Dutch:

> "We beg to announce that we have formed an association with Mr. E. Van Dien, accountant, Heerengracht 127, B/D Bergstraat, Amsterdam, Holland to represent us in accounting matters entrusted to our care in Holland and certain other European countries."

In 1929 this relationship was given a more formal basis in an understanding as to practice in Holland, Belgium, and Scandinavia.

As part of the expanding world-wide practice, agreements were entered into in 1932 with Ford, Rhodes and Harris and Ford, Rhodes and Davis of Australia as to practice there. In 1951 this evolved into Harris, Horne, Haskins & Sells, and eventually to Deloitte, Plender, Haskins & Sells. Agreements were also entered into in 1929 with Watkins, Hull, Wheeler & Johnston in New Zealand, Russell & Co. in Alexandria, Cairo, Athens, and other cities in the Mid-east, Ford, Rhodes & Parks and Ford, Rhodes & Thornton in India and Ceylon, and Ford, Rhodes, Robson, Morrow in Pakistan. In more recent years, relationships have been established with Sycip, Gorres, Velayo & Co. in the Philippines and other areas of the Far East, Turquand, Youngs & Co. in Malaysia, Robson, Morrow & Co. in Nepal, and Bainbridge, Caldwell, Ingram & Co. in the Bahamas.

Haskins & Sells is therefore qualified to represent American and other clients throughout the World.

At the beginning of World War II in addition to the practice offices of Deloitte, Plender, Haskins & Sells, Haskins & Sells had offices in Berlin, London, Paris, Manila, and Shanghai. These offices had serious problems due to war conditions, some of which are commented on hereafter.

At the time of the take-over in 1937 by the Japanese, the Manager of the Shanghai Office was William J. Fronk. He was followed in 1939 by Thomas H. Koerner, who had served in Berlin and later as Manager of the Paris Office.

At first the Japanese cooperated with the international group, but little by little their control tightened. Following the declaration of war in December 1941, the Japanese took over the International Settlement, and business practically ceased. Shortly before the War the office was engaged to make an audit of the accounts of the Shanghai Municipal Council (the Municipal Administration of the International Settlement), and had just completed the report on the audit early in December 1941. The Japanese, who had taken over the operation of the Council, requested that the report be rendered to them. This request was refused as they were not our clients. The unrendered report may still be with the working papers of the office, which were stored with a Danish businessman.

One of the last engagements of the Shanghai Office was for an American importer of machinery, 80% of whose assets consisted of silver and copper bars and coins, which were stored by the client in the street floor of a public warehouse (or "Go-Down") in the International Settlement. The client was reluctant to have us take a physical inventory, the manager stating he would confirm it. However, he eventually yielded to our insistence and Mr. Koerner and one of his staff with an employee of the client visited the warehouse to survey the situation. They found the premises consisted of about 15,000 square feet with approximately 1,500 cases and thousands of what appeared to be copper and silver bars. The lack of any adequate control made Mr. Koerner suspicious. Prior to the day of the physical inventory, for which he planned to use four of the staff and fifteen coolies, he received a visit from a man who warned him that if we proceeded it would be very unhealthy for Mr. Koerner and his men. Nevertheless, the next morning they went to the warehouse where the copper and silver bars were stacked in rows, forty bars high and forty bars deep. Mr. Koerner scratched the outside of some of the bars, which revealed what appeared to be copper and silver. He had the coolies remove the first row of bars and making a test found that all but the first rows consisted of cement bars painted to resemble silver and copper. He next proceeded to an inspection of the coin cases, three feet long, two feet high and one foot deep. An inspection showed coins in the first row of cases but gravel in all the others.

On leaving the warehouse, Mr. Koerner was met by two International Settlement Police, who said they were assigned to guard him to his home. On his arrival there he found another International Settlement policeman to be his bodyguard for an indefinite period of time. Inquiry developed that Mr. Koerner's friend, the Police Commissioner, had the warehouse under surveillance and that one of the men who had access to it had been fished out of the Whangpoo river with his throat cut from ear to ear. Mr. Koerner reported the findings orally to the client, who was afraid to do anything about it because of the ominous situation in Shanghai. No formal report was rendered. The only aftermath of the incident occurred a week later. Mr. Koerner just stepped out of his room at the office for a moment, when he heard the sound of a shot and found a hole in the window and a bullet hole in the wall opposite his desk.

The office was closed July 1942, but continued to do a small amount of work for the subsequent four months. Mr. Koerner was successful in avoiding arrest, but was frequently interrogated by the Japanese in the infamous Bridge House, the Japanese prison. He did not suffer any physical torture, but the method and extent of the interrogations were mental torture. The Koerners were evacuated with the second exchange of prisoners, which began September 23, 1943.

When tensions developed in the Pacific in 1941, the partner in charge of the Manila Office, Vernon Thompson, was authorized November 12 by cable to return his wife and children. However, Mr. Thompson doubted there would be a war between Japan and the United States and action was delayed.

When war was declared on December 7, 1941, there was not time to evacuate the American personnel as the Japanese attacked the Philippines and occupied Manila on January 2, 1942.

Vernon Thompson and his wife and two children were interned in Santo Tomas prison camp, and R. W. Diehl and his wife in the Los Banos prison camp. They were returned to the United States in June 1945, very much underweight, but in reasonably good health. Mr. and Mrs. Carey were also interned in Santo Tomas prison camp, returning in June 1945.

The difficult experiences of Mr. Carey did not deter him from returning to the Far East in 1954 and becoming partner in charge of the Tokyo Office for five years. He was transferred to Honolulu in 1959 to take charge of the practice in the Hawaiian Islands, but on his retirement he returned to the Tokyo Office on a consulting basis.

The Manila Office was not reopened—at first because of conditions in Manila, but later because of restrictions of the Philippine Government on foreign accountants.

Prior to the Second World War, the Paris Office had some interesting experiences.

In 1932, when Mr. Lovibond was in Berlin, we were asked to consider making an audit of the enterprises of Ivar Kreuger the Swedish financier, often called the match king. These were the Swedish Match Company, which controlled 250 factories in forty-three countries, and Kreuger & Toll Company, which had become one of the largest and most important financial institutions in Europe making loans to impoverished governments in return for industrial concessions. Mr. Lovibond talked with some of the officials of the companies and outlined some of the steps we considered necessary. He was requested to go to Paris to see Mr. Kreuger, and an appointment was made for March 12, 1932. Kreuger had presumably been advised of our audit plan and realizing that the falsification of accounts and the forging of bonds would be uncovered he committed suicide in the Paris hotel the morning of the appointment. The Kreuger Company subsequently went into bankruptcy.

When Mr. Koerner was Manager in Paris in the thirties, he was visited by an emissary of King Carol of Romania and asked to meet the King at Hotel George V regarding an audit of oil by-products bought by a Boston company. Because of the difficulty in taking or supervising inventories in Romania at that time, it was pointed out to the King that an audit without this would be useless to him. The King was understanding and the visit was a cordial one.

When war was declared in Europe September 1, 1939, the Manager of the Paris Office was Paul Bohus, who had been transferred from Berlin on January 1, 1938. We endeavored to have Mr. Bohus return to the United States, but he felt he could continue in Paris. After the occupation of Paris by the Germans in 1940, the office continued to operate under difficulties although life for foreigners was not too bad. The office was finally closed under instructions from New York in November 1941, and Mr. Bohus was able with great difficulty to escape and returned to the United States June 30, 1942.

After the War, the Paris Office was reopened.

The Berlin Office was opened November 1, 1924 with Edward A. Kracke temporarily as Resident Partner and Arthur M. Lovibond as Manager (later partner). Conditions in Berlin became difficult under Adolph Hitler, and in December 1935 Mr. Lovibond was moved to London.

Following the close of the War, the office was reopened in Dusseldorf and now operates as Deloitte, Plender, Haskins & Sells, Wirtschaftsprufungsgesellschaft, mbH.

On the inception of war in Europe September 1, 1939 the partner in charge of the London Office was Arthur M. Lovibond. He remained in London until June 30, 1940, when he returned to New York. The office continued to operate with staff above the "reserved age," although always shorthanded. Reports came through regularly from the office with typical British understatement dealing only with client and staff matters. Work occupied their time in the day and much of the night was spent patrolling the roofs as fire watchers. It was only after the War that we learned that a number of bombs fell within a block of the office and one hit a loaded bus on the street just in front of the office building.

The office continued in operation all during and after the War.

After the War, the rehabilitation and reorganization of the international practice was assigned to Percy R. Everett. He first gave attention to London, Paris and Germany, then to other areas, all with much success.

Percy R. Everett was born in London, England in 1892 and was educated in English private schools. His father was Assistant General Manager of Thos. Cook & Son, and Mr. Everett's early employment was in the European offices of that Company. He served in the British Army in World War I from 1914 until discharged for medical reasons in 1916.

He came to the United States in 1916, and served briefly with Haskins & Sells in New York before joining this Country's war effort with the United States Shipping Board. He was retained on the Firm's payroll at $1.00 a year and returned to Haskins & Sells in 1921.

In 1925 he became a Manager in the Firm's 44th Street Office in New York. He was a man of towering physique and colleagues recall the deep impression his integrity made on clients. He was frequently

After World War II, Percy R. Everett reconstructed the Firm's European practice. Its growth accelerated under his direction with the combining there of the practices of H&S and Deloittes.

called upon to arbitrate differences among conflicting parties. In one instance in a brokerage firm, where serious differences arose among some of the partners, Mr. Everett acted as arbitrator to the lasting satisfaction of the parties involved. In 1940, when the Georgia Warm Springs polio resort founded by Franklin Delano Roosevelt was without a manager, Mr. Everett managed the organization on a part-time basis until 1945.

In 1944 he was made responsible for reorganizing the Firm's London and Paris offices, and then for coordinating the Firm's international practice both administratively and technically. From that time on, he traveled extensively in Europe, South America, Africa, Australia, and New Zealand in connection with the consolidation and extension of the practice of the Firm. Under his direction Haskins & Sells accelerated the extension of its practice abroad in conjunction with the long established firm of Deloitte, Plender, Griffiths & Co., and he helped materially in the program of combining the practices of the two firms outside of England.

He was active in the Pilgrims of the United States, and was Chairman of the Finance Committee of the St. George's Society, but his hobby was sailing and he was an honorary life member of the Larchmont Yacht Club, of which he was a trustee and Treasurer, and was a member of the Sarasota (Florida) Yacht Club. He died on November 15, 1969.

On Mr. Everett's retirement in 1955, he was succeeded by J. Harry Williams, who was born in Daingerfield, Texas in 1901, and graduated from the University of Texas in 1926 with the degree of B.B.A. He came with Haskins & Sells in 1927 in Dallas, going to Houston in 1937 where he became Manager in 1938, and partner in 1939. He then came to General Practice in the Executive Office for several years, then to the New York Broad Street Office, and in 1947 became Partner in Charge of the St. Louis Office, remaining until 1955. His supervision of the foreign practice for the next ten years was a period of great growth and development, necessitating much international travel. On his retirement he was succeeded by Charles L. Clapp, but continued to render helpful service in the foreign fields. Prior to his retirement, he served for several years on the International Relations Committee of the American Institute of Accountants, was on the Board of Directors of the American Turkish Society, and was a member of a number of international organizations, including The

J. Harry Williams, after extensive responsibilities with the Firm in the United States, succeeded Mr. Everett in the supervision of the international practice during a decade of great growth and development.

Japan Society, The African Affairs Society, The Pan American Society, and the American Australian Association. The international practice did not give him time for community activities in New York, but in St. Louis he served on the Board of Trustees of the Saint Louis Country Day School, The Health and Hospital Budget Committee of the Saint Louis Community Chest, and was on the St. Louis Planning Council, serving as Chairman of the Special Committee to Investigate Hospital Facilities in Saint Louis.

With the closer relations with Deloitte, Plender, Griffiths & Co. in 1952, the London Office of Haskins & Sells was merged with Deloittes, and the offices of the two firms in Paris were eventually consolidated into one—as Deloitte, Plender, Haskins & Sells. Offices of Deloitte, Plender, Haskins & Sells were opened in Brussels in 1952, in Tokyo in 1954, in Caracas in 1955, Milan in 1957, Bogota in 1959, Zurich in 1961, Medellin in 1962, Cali, Rome, and Geneva in 1963, Madrid and Osaka in 1964, Barcelona in 1965, Guayaquil and Panama City in 1966, Cordoba, Copenhagen, and Lisbon in 1968, and Hannover, Luxembourg, and Oslo in 1969.

Canadian Practice

Deloitte, Plender, Griffiths, & Co. conducted its practice in Canada through an office in Montreal, which was opened in 1912. Haskins & Sells' practice in Canada prior to 1924 was handled through its offices in the United States, chiefly New York and Detroit. In 1924 these practices were combined in the copartnership of Deloitte, Plender, Haskins & Sells. At that time, Gordon Tansley was the Manager of the Montreal Office. He resigned in 1931, and was succeeded briefly by Campbell G. McConnell (until 1931), and then by Kenneth W. Dalglish.

With expansion in the practice in Canada an office was opened in Toronto in 1930 through the merger in that City of the practice of William J. Saunders and William A. Cameron, and to take care of the practice on the West Coast an office was opened in Vancouver in 1953.

In that year Kenneth W. Dalglish, who was the Senior Partner in Canada, resigned to go into private work, and Colonel Andrew Stewart went from New York to Toronto to establish a Head Office there for Canada, and became the Senior Partner in Canada. Colonel Stewart was a Chartered Accountant of Scotland and a Chartered Accountant of Ontario, in addition to being a Certified Public Accountant. He became acquainted with Walter J. Macdonald, of Millar, Macdonald & Co. of Winnipeg, Manitoba, who was then President of the Canadian Institute of Chartered Accountants. As a result, discussions between John W. Queenan and Mr. Macdonald were held and a merger of Millar, Macdonald & Co. and Deloitte, Plender, Haskins & Sells (Canada) was arranged and consummated in 1954, after the close of Mr. Macdonald's term as President.

Mr. Macdonald became the Senior Partner of Deloitte, Plender, Haskins & Sells in Canada, and through his wide acquaintance and wise and aggressive leadership mergers were arranged with Rooke, Thomas & Company of Regina, Saskatchewan in 1955, Paisley, Wallace & Co. of Vancouver, Prince George, and Quensel in 1955, and Patriquin, Duncan, McClary McClary & Company of Edmonton, Alberta in 1956. Offices were opened in Calgary in 1957, and Windsor in 1956, the latter through the merger of Macdonald & Healy.

The tragic death of Walter Macdonald of a heart attack on November 24, 1959 was a great loss to the Canadian firm. The Canadian Chartered Accountant in January 1969 paid the following tribute to him:

> "On November 24, 1959 Walter J. Macdonald, F.C.A. of Winnipeg, died of a heart attack in Montreal at the age of 65. To those who trained and worked under him and to the great number of chartered accountants across the country who recognized his many admirable qualities, his sudden passing leaves a gap that can never be filled. By reason of his record of public service and the respect with which he was regarded in business and service organizations, he stands out as an example to his profession of what a chartered accountant has to offer his community.
>
> Walter Macdonald was born in Glasgow and, as a young man of 19, moved with his family to Winnipeg in 1913, qualifying as a Canadian chartered accountant in 1915. In that year he enlisted as a private in the 44th Battalion of the Canadian Expeditionary Force and, shortly after, went overseas with his unit. He rose to the rank of Captain and won the Military Medal and Military Cross and Bar.
>
> In 1920 he established the firm of Millar, Macdonald & Company in Winnipeg which in 1954 was to become associated with Deloitte, Plender, Haskins & Sells. He was the senior partner of the firm at the time of his death. At an early period in

his career he evinced a keen interest in the affairs of his profession and in 1931 and 1932 was elected president of the Institute of Chartered Accountants of Manitoba. During the next 25 years he served on numerous Institute committees and was on the Executive of the Canadian Institute for four years before becoming its president in 1953. During his term of office the concept of the Institute annual meeting was changed to give wider recognition to the problems of the accountant in public practice and particularly the accountant in industry.

Walter Macdonald gave a great deal of time to serving the youth of his community and from 1949 to 1954 he was president of the Winnipeg Y.M.C.A. Church work had long been one of his special interests. He was a member of the Board of Regents of United College and general chairman of the United College Appeal Fund. The list of his offices, committee appointments and the commissions on which he served are too numerous to list.

He will be remembered as a man of vision and foresight with a great capacity for hard work who also retained the personal touch and an earnest solicitude for the interests of his clients. His warmth and fierce loyalty, characteristic of the Highland Scot, gained him many friends. He was devoted to his profession and by his endeavors he left an imprint on Canadian accounting that will never be erased."

The successor to Mr. Macdonald as Senior Partner in 1960 was Clement L. King, who had become a partner in Deloitte, Plender, Haskins & Sells in 1955, after having served as Secretary and Research Director of the Canadian Institute of Chartered Accountants. Mr. King was killed in 1965 in the crash of the Canadian Pacific Airliner, while enroute from Vancouver to Prince George. He was succeeded as Senior Partner by James G. Duncan, who had been Senior Partner of Patriquin, Duncan, McClary, McClary & Company of Edmonton at the time of its merger in 1956.

Additional offices were opened in Hamilton, Ontario in 1959 and Oshawa, Ontario in 1965.

The partners of Deloitte, Plender, Haskins & Sells (Canada) have had a distinguished record of serving the profession as is evidenced by the following:

Walter J. Macdonald

President of the Institute of Chartered Accountants of Manitoba

1929-1931
President of the Canadian Institute of Chartered Accountants 1953-1954
James G. Duncan
President of the Institute of Chartered Accountants of Alberta
1948-1949
Kenneth W. Dalglish
President of the Dominion Association of Chartered Accountants 1939-1940
(now the Canadian Institute of Chartered Accountants)
President of the Institute of Chartered Accountants of
Province of Quebec 1935-1936
John P. McClary
President of the Institute of Chartered Accountants of Alberta
1956-1957
Harold S. Moffet
President of the Institute of Chartered Accountants of Saskatchewan
1951-1952
Harry O. Patriquin
President of the Institute of Chartered Accountants of Alberta 1925-1926
W. Givens Smith
President of the Institute of Chartered Accountants of Saskatchewan
1944-1945
President of the Canadian Institute of Chartered Accountants 1956-1957
Reginald R. Thomas
President of the Institute of Chartered Accountants of Saskatchewan
1934-1936
William M. Vicars
President of the Institute of Chartered Accountants of Saskatchewan
1948-1949

There are 72 partners in the Canadian firm, four directors, and 44 principals. Annual meetings of the partners have been held usually at a resort hotel beginning with one in Minaki, Ontario in 1955.

There are close relations between Haskins & Sells and the Canadian firm with exchanges of technical material, programs, questionnaires, procedures, MAS, and Auditape information. Many of the Canadian partners have attended meetings of Haskins & Sells' partners from 1933 on, and partners of Haskins & Sells have attended the meetings of the Canadian partners from the time they were instituted by Mr. Macdonald in 1955.

14

Technical and Organizational Development in the Firm—
Everett J. Shifflett—Electronic Data Processing—
Management Advisory Services—Statistical Sampling—
Auditape—Haskins & Sells Internal Accounting—
H&S Reports—Meetings

In 1954 in the very early days of electronic equipment, a group of twenty-six partners and principals was organized by Everett J. Shifflett to visit plants of and attend instructional courses given by companies manufacturing electronic equipment, so as to give these men a basic understanding of electronic data processing equipment.

Mr. Shifflett was another of the college graduates brought into the firm by John R. Wildman. He came to Mr. Wildman's attention in 1928 through Professor Fayette H. Elwell of The University of Wisconsin, who spoke of Shifflett as one of his best accounting majors graduating that year. After several months training in the Technical Procedure Department, he was assigned to the New York Broad Street Office. In 1936 he was transferred to General Practice in the Executive Office. He made rapid progress, becoming a Temporary Principal in 1936, a Principal in 1938, and a Partner June 1, 1939. Transferred to the New York uptown office, he remained there until August 1, 1952, spending the major part of 1943-1948 in tax work and handling with great skill and with warmly efficient client relations many important engagements.

On his return in 1952 to the Executive Office he took over the top supervision of the General Motors engagement, visiting plants (and our offices) in South America in 1954, in Europe in 1955, and South Africa and Australia in 1956.

During this period he continued the development and dissemination of electronic data processing information, preparing, in collaboration with Gordon C. Stubbs, two brochures which were the earliest of their kind in the accounting profession: Data Processing by Electronics,

Everett J. Shifflett, an early master of electronic data processing, organized the Firm's Management Advisory Services as "an array of ideas and techniques designed to help clients to be more effective—to do a better job."

1955, and Introduction to Data Processing, 1957. These were followed later by three additional brochures for which Mr. Shifflett was chielfy responsible: Operations Research 1958; Internal Control in Electronic Accounting Systems 1965; and Administrative Controls in Business Operations 1966; together with the book Processing Securities Transactions 1969. He organized and edited The Pension System in the United States in 1964, a publication which was very favorably received in insurance circles. Also, he originated the publication of the Haskins & Sells Selected Papers and edited the first issue.

One of the interesting engagements in which Mr. Shifflett wrote the report was on the examination of the accounting records of President Lyndon B. Johnson, Mrs. Johnson, and their two daughters for the period from January 1, 1954 to July 31, 1964. The report was made public by the President—the first time this had ever been done in the case of such a report. It was reproduced in full in The New York Times and widely commented upon in the news media in the United States and various foreign countries.

Mr. Shifflett also testified in various public utility rate cases, an echo of the days when Mr. Ludlam testified in important utility cases in Missouri and Oklahoma.

Mr. Shifflett served on a number of Committees of the American Institute of Certified Public Accountants and was Chairman for two years of the Committee on Relations with the Securities and Exchange Commission and the Stock Exchanges, working closely with the Securities and Exchange Commission on important releases.

Until his retirement in 1965, Mr. Shifflett also handled all of the "trouble" cases of the Firm, working closely with our offices, with our legal counsel, with Saul Levy (then the leading authority in the United States on accountants' liability), and with the counsel and representatives of our insurers. This is an area that receives little publicity and his protection of the Firm in these matters was outstanding. Even after his retirement he continued to assist the Firm with wise counsel and testimony.

Mr. Shifflett also organized the Management Advisory Services of Haskins & Sells, planning the organization, engaging specialists, and training Haskins & Sells men to function in this area. He established the policy of serving our clients as consultants in Management Advisory Services and of involving the client personnel in this work.

In an early memorandum Mr. Shifflett reminded those interested and engaged in Management Advisory Services that while at that time these services seemed to be a new activity, actually the current program was only a continuation and expansion of service long rendered by the Firm and the profession as a whole. He then cited the extract from a citation issued in 1895 to the two founding members of the Firm by a Joint Commission of Congress which is set forth earlier in this history.

Mr. Shifflett went on to say that MAS is essentially an array of ideas and techniques designed to help people to be more effective—to do a better job. Gordon L. Murray, who took over the responsibilities of coordinating the Management Advisory Services, also emphasized this by saying it involved the application of techniques we already know to more areas of a business and acquiring capability in entirely new techniques, and that our Management Advisory Services exist to help client management make more effective—more profitable—decisions through the application of appropriate modern management techniques. We serve as consultants. We largely provide know-how rather than manpower and we expect client personnel to participate in the work. In this way, they become fully qualified to carry on once our participation is concluded. The consulting approach, in the degree we apply it, is somewhat unique among consulting and accounting firms providing such services. It sets us somewhat apart and has been well received by clients. The approach is most consistent with the Firm's independence as accountants.

The development of Statistical Sampling in Auditing evolved from the need for a more objective basis for determining the extent of audit tests of accounting records. At the outset of an assignment for reviewing and updating the Firm's auditing procedures, Kenneth W. Stringer recognized this need and also identified some mathematical and practical problems inherent in the traditional sampling plans available at that time. After several years of study and consultation with Professor Frederick F. Stephan of Princeton University, they developed and introduced early in the 1960s the special H & S Sampling Plan that is used so extensively in our audit practice today. The principal mathematical feature that distinguishes this plan from those previously available is its capability to provide rigorous reliability and monetary precision limits even though samples may include few if any monetary errors, which is often the case in auditing applications. The flexibility and ease of application by auditors is another outstanding feature of this plan.

Mr. Stringer's concern for improved auditing procedures led to another pioneering contribution—the Haskins & Sells Auditape System. With the increasing use of computers for maintaining business records, the need for better methods for applying the Firm's Statistical Sampling as well as other auditing procedures to such records became increasingly apparent. In the fall of 1964 Mr. Stringer arranged for the initial work on this critical project and early in 1965 recruited a team of computer-oriented accountants to concentrate their efforts on it. By September of that year the new Haskins & Sells Auditape System was unveiled. This System is a set of generalized computer programs that can be used on computer records in virtually any format, requiring no special programming by the auditor and only minimal training for its use. Because of the simplicity and versatility inherent in the System it can serve as the "key to the computer" for audit and management personnel who are not data-processing specialists.

Although developed primarily for our audit purpose, the Auditape System was recognized as a potentially useful management tool, particularly when special data needed for management decisions is not available from regular reports or existing computer programs. For this reason, Haskins & Sells introduced its Auditape System to its clients in the fall of 1966 through a series of regional meetings and made it available for their use.

The Auditape System was presented at the Annual Meeting of the AICPA in 1967 and made available to the entire profession at that time. Following this meeting the Firm conducted a series of Auditape training courses for the AICPA as a means of encouraging CPAs to take advantage of this breakthrough in computer auditing procedures. Since that time several other accounting firms have developed their own systems to serve purposes similar to those of Auditape.

Haskins & Sells has been in the forefront of the computer revolution. In the mid 1950s the Firm published two introductory booklets on electronic data processing (EDP). They are still in today's literature and in demand by clients and teachers. One of them was made a part of an EDP course for the American Institute of CPAs. The Firm also published "Internal Control in Electronic Accounting Systems," which was made a part of the Firm's EDP home-study course. Haskins & Sells offices have been using EDP on audit engagements for many years with very satisfactory results.

Haskins & Sells was the first of the larger accounting firms to put its own internal accounting on the computer.

A brief review of the internal accounting procedures is interesting. During the early years of the Firm, the bookkeeping requirements were relatively simple although at all times the accounting was centralized in the New York Office and later in the Executive Office.

By 1927, the year Mr. Queenan was employed, the entire Financial Department consisted of only nineteen employees. The Data Processing Department consisted of one adding machine. Subsequently, the Data Processing Department was expanded to include a "Millionaire" calculator, which looked, sounded and acted like a Rube Goldberg creation. At one time, the New York Broad Street Office used a primitive IBM sorter for brokerage work. However, this machine made so much noise and vibration that the tenants on the floor below insisted that the machine be disposed of. It was only in the late 1930s that the old-fashioned high bookkeeping desks and high stools used in the Financial Department were replaced with oak desks and chairs. Some of these high desks and stools were still in use when Aubrey Stewart was transferred to the Financial Department in 1946 and succeeded Jennie Palen as head of the department.

The year 1947 was a year of many changes in the Financial Department. Arthur B. Foye became the Ranking Partner of the Firm on June 1, 1947. That year the first system change was made, and the client ledgers were redesigned to provide for the posting of client charges in hours only and converting the total to dollars at the end of each month. In order to control the monthly earnings by offices, a Sunstrand accounting machine was purchased. The Sunstrand was so helpful that a second machine was purchased to prepare the semimonthly payroll since the normal preparation was getting difficult for the two payroll clerks. Another first in 1947 was the purchase of a check signing machine to sign the many payroll checks which previously were signed by one or more retired partners.

After 1947 the Firm began a period of rapid growth. In an effort to keep pace with the increased volume of data transactions, a systems study under Aubrey Stewart resulted in placing a formal order with IBM in 1951 for one 402 acounting machine and six keypunch machines and some auxiliary IBM equipment. The IBM machines were delivered in April and May 1952, and the system became operational in June.

It was no easy task to change from hand records to punched card records. The existing alphabetic control had to be changed to numerical control. Partners and employees were given identification numbers. Offices, clients and engagements were given numbers. People resisted the regimentation of numerical reporting. Mr. Coursen, the partner in charge of New York Office, had serious doubts that the new system would work so he maintained duplicate accounting records for New York during the first year of the new system. When all the differences were found to be errors in the New York duplicate records, Mr. Coursen finally accepted the new system.

It was fortunate that punched-card accounting was adopted in 1952, because the McLaren merger became effective in June of that year and the Deloitte merger became effective in October. It would have been a formidable task to take care of the additional merger volume with hand records. In 1951 there was established the Firm's non-contributory group life insurance plan, and in 1952 a contributory group life insurance plan was added. All of these changes resulted in the necessity for the establishment of an IBM payroll system which finally became operational in May 1953. Over the years the IBM unit record equipment was gradually increased until there were two shifts operating on the accounting machines and the related auxiliary equipment.

The Firm's growth continued rapidly during the 1960s with the result that the Financial Department, particularly Data Processing, had a task to keep pace. In 1960 the three IBM 402 accounting machines were replaced with three high speed IBM 407s. In 1962, a regular night shift was added. In 1964, a fourth IBM 407 accounting machine was put into operation.

With the increasing volume of data, the days of one unit machines were numbered. The first computer was installed in October of 1965. The Honeywell H-200 replaced most of the IBM equipment. In 1967, a fourth tape drive for the H-200 was added. In 1968, the computer workday was extended from 8 hours to 12 hours. It was still difficult to keep pace, so that in December of 1969 there was installed a Honeywell H-125 computer to supplement the H-200. The new Honeywell H-125 has the same configurations as the H-200, except it operates at about one-half the speed of the H-200. It is necessary to operate both computers on a two shift basis.

Plans for 1971 envisage new equipment to handle the increasing volume. The introduction of these modern ideas took much study, but are part of the determination of the Firm to be in the forefront of technological advance.

"H & S Reports" was started on a quarterly basis in the Autumn of 1963 to keep the members of the organization informed as to events and developments in the Firm and in its relation to the profession. The Haskins & Sells Bulletin issued from 1918 to 1932 tended to deal chiefly with technical matters, but "H & S Reports" had a broader purpose: "to clarify for each of us the vision of what we are building—to remind us of our common goals." Instead of brief notes as to partners and principals, a great deal of space has been devoted to all of the people in the organization. While the Haskins & Sells Bulletins had few pictures, the "H & S Reports" has made extensive use of photographs of people and places. The difference in format of the Bulletin and the "H & S Reports" is a striking indication of the change in the public image of the accounting profession and the great development in the art of communication.

Interesting and informative articles on Haskins & Sells offices have been featured in the "Reports." During the period from the Autumn of 1963 to the Spring of 1969, articles appeared on twenty offices with a wide knowledge of the people in them and the clients. Pictures and some brief biographies of all of the new partners and directors, principals and managers have been included. The new CPAs have been listed, and a record of over 2,300 articles and speeches by Haskins & Sells people has been shown.

Thoughtful memorials of Weldon Powell, General Arthur H. Carter, Clem King, and Sir Russell Kettle told of these men, their accomplishments and their human qualities. Articles on Japan, Latin and South America have given interesting views of the Countries and our work in them. Some of our clients have been featured in articles.

In addition, there have been many broad articles on professional matters such as the Accounting Principles Board, Accounting Principles and the Investment Credit, Inventories, Professional Development, the "Great Money Controversy," and the Report on the Common Body of Knowledge. Special departments and techniques have been reported on: International Practice, Taxes, Management Advisory Services, Auditape, Personnel, and Research.

All of the articles have been lucidly written and wherever possible fully illustrated. The "H & S Reports" has been accomplishing its original purposes and more.

Meetings

Over the long history of the Firm annual meetings of the partners and directors and principals and managers have brought them in close touch with each other, and have made possible face-to-face discussion of management practices and policies, professional and technical matters, and plans for growth and development.

The practice started early, for following the death of Mr. Haskins early in 1903 Mr. Sells felt the need of the full support of the partners and managers and brought them together each year.

These meetings have continued annually except for the years of the First and Second World Wars and a depression year. In 1946 the number of partners and managers necessitated separate meetings for the partners and for the managers. In 1953 the practice was established of having meetings of the partners and directors and their wives every four years, and in 1956 the same practice was adopted for the principals and managers and their wives. Appendix B lists the years and locations of these meetings and mentions other meetings held.

There were two major purposes in holding these meetings. One was to bring the partners and later their wives together so that they would become well acquainted with each other, and thus help to build a strong and warm esprit de corps, and develop friendly inter-office relations. The other major purpose was to review Firm policies; to inform the partners on the Firm's financial affairs; to discuss legal liabilities of accountants and related "trouble cases"; to exchange views on public and client relations, new business and staff recruitment; to refresh the minds of the partners on current technical and professional developments and emphasize the Firm's advancements in them; and to acquaint the partners with the practice abroad, its importance and its problems. The latter was supplemented by bringing to the meetings various partners of Deloitte, Plender, Haskins & Sells throughout the world and of other affiliated firms in Holland, Germany, Philippines, and New Zealand.

The meetings with the wives, both of the partners and directors and principals and managers, were also extremely helpful in making acquaintances and building friendships with great benefit to morale. The wives skillfully organized their parts in the meetings with many participating in activity and hospitality committees and in fascinating hobby shows.

15

Partners with Fifty Years Service

So many partners have made great contributions to the growth, development, and success of Haskins & Sells that it is difficult to avoid mentioning each and every one for over all of its history it has been a closely knit, warmly cooperative team. A list of the partners and the dates of admission to the Firm, and their death or resignation is appended.

There are ten partners who have over fifty years of service with the Firm:

Charles C. Croggon
Orion N. Hutchinson
Arthur B. Foye
James M. Cashin
Edmund A. Clarke
Gordon M. Hill
Ralph W. Peters
Robert L. Reamy
Loy J. Case
Vernon Thompson

While much could be written about the service in widespread areas of these "fifty year" men, comment on three of them will indicate the varied and dedicated activities of all of them.

Charles C. Croggon came with Haskins & Sells in Baltimore in 1915 at the age of twenty-nine, following twelve years in private accounting work. This was, as Mr. Croggon has said, in the days when the accountant was "on his own." There were few rules or procedures and the accountant going out on an audit was given a simple engagement memorandum and expected to make the examination using his common sense based on his experience and write a good report. He also had to try to make sure that there were no frauds or defalcations, for this was one of the most important features of the work of accountants at that time. Mr. Croggon as a result developed a "second sense" as to frauds and uncovered many of them.

He made progress, being appointed Manager in 1919 and a Partner in 1922 in charge of the Baltimore Office. He developed a wide acquaintance with the business leaders and educators in Maryland, and did much to develop the accountants in the Baltimore Office, pressing them to secure their CPA degrees. In this office during the active service of Mr. Croggon, ten partners were given their early training: Raymond C. Reik, Orion N. Hutchinson, Thomas V. Barb, Robert L. Reamy, Hunter Ashlin Dykes, William B. Tittsworth, Raymond E. North, William C. Witler, George E. Babylon, Jr., and Warren K. Reed.

His activity in the Maryland Society of Certified Public Accountants is evident in the list of State Societies Presidents, where Maryland had eight, which is more than any other office.

Gordon M. Hill's entrance into Haskins & Sells was in 1917, when he was 23 years old, after attending Georgia Institute of Technology and several years of private accounting work. Under conditions at that time, accountants were often employed on a temporary basis, when work for them was available. This was so for Mr. Hill and he was a temporary employee for two months from February 12 to April 7. After a further period of private work and some professional accounting for one of the oldest and most distinguished of Georgia accountants, James Respess, he returned to the Atlanta office of Haskins & Sells on a permanent basis on January 1, 1919 as a junior accountant.

The Manager of the Atlanta Office, L. C. Matthews, was called to New York for consultation in September 1919 leaving the office in charge of the junior accountant. An emergency engagement arose from an Atlanta bank, necessitating an immediate report, and Mr. Hill did the work, wrote, signed, and delivered the report—breaking the rule that no report could go out without review in New York and the rule as to only a manager or partner signing a report. Incidentally, he also rendered and collected the bill. On Mr. Matthews return, he was so impressed by the way Mr. Hill had handled the situation that he secured his change to Senior Accountant with the comment "Good work, diplomacy and discretion under trying circumstances and

Charles C. Croggon, partner in charge of the Baltimore Office from 1922 to 1954, practiced in a day when there were few rules and procedures and the auditor was "on his own."

More than fifty years ago, Gordon M. Hill was commended for "good work, diplomacy and discretion under trying circumstances and initiative displayed while in charge of office in absence of Manager."

initiative displayed while in charge of office in absence of Manager." These were the characteristics Mr. Hill displayed throughout his life with the Firm.

With the growing importance of income and profits taxes, Mr. Hill was transferred to New Orleans in 1920 to assist in tax work, after a refresher course of six weeks in New York. In New Orleans he became a Supervisory Accountant in 1921, and Assistant Manager in 1925.

When the Jacksonville Office was opened February 15, 1926, Mr. Hill was made Manager, remaining until 1931. Golf was always one of his great interests, and he developed his game in Jacksonville, making a hole in one in June 1930 on the Florida Country Club course.

In recognition of his talents he was transferred to the Executive Office December 11, 1931 to take charge of the General Motors engagement in Detroit. His three years there completed, he returned to General Practice work in the Executive Office in 1934, becoming a principal at that time, and a partner in 1935. He went to the New York 40th Street Office in 1938, and in 1949 was in charge of that office. He commenced his retirement in 1954, but undertook top supervision of the General Motors engagement in 1957, in the course of which he visited the General Motors units around the world.

His interest in golf grew, and he became a Director and then President of the United States Seniors' Golf Association, participating in eight of their international tournaments in Canada, England, and Scotland, and in a great many tournaments in the United States. He also was one of the founders and became the Second Vice President of the Long Island Senior Golf Association, and President of the Three Score and Ten Club (for golfers over 70). While golf gave Mr. Hill much pleasure, the many and excellent contacts he made in it were most helpful to the Firm.

Another of his interests was music, and he was a Director of the Metropolitan Opera Association, Assistant Treasurer and then Treasurer. He did much to organize and improve the accounting of the Association, and was one of the few who could differ with the Director, Rudolph Bing, and retain his respect and his friendship.

Mr. Hill was long a Director and Treasurer of the Union League Club (New York), and was President of the Circumnavigators Club, an organization of those who had circumnavigated the earth.

Orion N. Hutchinson was born in Harborton, Virginia November

Orion N. Hutchinson, a civic and religious leader in Charlotte, was responsible for the development and growth of the H&S office from its opening there in 1926 until his retirement from active practice in 1950.

3, 1889, and attended High School there, and took Graduate Accounting at Eastman College in Poughkeepsie, New York. He was in accounting work for Liggett & Myers Tobacco Company from December 1911 to July 1917, when he was employed in the Baltimore Office of Haskins & Sells. Undoubtedly, his acquaintance with the Company's affairs and its people was helpful to him in securing the Liggett & Myers engagement for the Firm.

He made rapid progress in Baltimore, becoming an in-charge accountant in 1918, a supervisory accountant in 1919, and Assistant Manager in 1924. When the Charlotte Office was opened in 1926, he was made Manager of it, and became a partner there in 1931.

Mr. Hutchinson was active in professional affairs, holding Certificates in North Carolina, South Carolina, Tennessee, and Maryland. He served as Vice President and then President of the North Carolina Association of Certified Public Acountants, and as a Vice President of the American Society of Certified Public Accountants. Following Mr. Ludlam's emphasis on good work and supplementing it by developing a wide acquaintance in the business community in North Carolina, he was responsible for the development and growth of the Charlotte Office.

16

The Future—by John W. Queenan

From the Firm's inception seventy-five years ago, the partners have been forward looking.

Charles Waldo Haskins, in an address to the New York Chapter of the Institute of Accountants on January 25, 1900, said:

> "As we aim at good work and high professional skill, as we exemplify a high standard of probity and honesty, as we illustrate the words of Montaigne that men should not live for themselves but for the public; so will we educate the public to understand and acknowledge this interdependent relation and more and more cordially welcome us to our place in the center of the system of trade and commerce."

A little later in an address before the Institute of Accountants in New York on June 27, 1901, he said:

> "Accountancy is a progressive science; and the trend of professional accountancy is upward; we have evidently heeded the Counsel of Ralph Waldo Emerson and have 'hitched our wagon to a star.' "

He amplified these thoughts in a subsequent address:

> "Aside from all personal interest in accountancy, I hold our common calling in the highest honor and admiration—not for its worthy record of achievement already past, but for the stupendous possibility within its grasp as one of the moral and educational forces of the modern world. Educationally as well as morally, the science of accountancy represents a power of which we are not as yet fully conscious. The well-being of the accountancy of tomorrow is, in very large measure, dependent upon the

> faithfulness of the mere handful of accountants who compose our profession today. Oneness of method and of professional aspirations, enlarged and exalted views of the worth and dignity of our calling, and a steady, studious and conscientious aim to discharge well our obligations to the business world will ensure to us that universal and permanent recognition upon which hang the hopes of higher accountancy."

The prophetic character of Haskins' words are evident to all of us today. The "mere handful of accountants" of his day have become a throng who have achieved wide recognition in the business community of today. For the past twenty-five years the profession has been meeting and coping with increasingly complex problems created by our rapidly developing society. This recognition and the reasonably satisfactory handling of these problems have been achieved not without criticism; recognition tends to spawn criticism. However, even under attack, the accounting profession has demonstrated that moral character prescribed by Charles Waldo Haskins.

Never before has our world changed so much or so fast as in the past few decades. We may think first of the glamorous achievements—the flying machine of the Wright brothers, the electronic marvels of yesterday which we accept as commonplace today, the harnessing of nuclear energy, the launching of satellites, and man's first trip to the moon.

There have been other changes—less glamorous, maybe, but equally important. The economic system, after having progressed at a relatively slow pace for centuries, has been revolutionized by the advancement of technology and by changes in industrial organizations and government activities. Many enterprises have come to rely on external capital and credit, which has separated ownership from management. Government services, taxation, and regulation of business have increased.

These developments have had a vital impact on the economy of the free world and on the progress of our profession. Accounting has become increasingly important for internal administration and control and for external financial reporting. In countries with a highly developed industry, the accounting profession has progressed from a small group of practitioners, concentrated in a few centers of population and unrecognized publicly, to a well-organized profession enjoying world-wide influence.

The fact that such stature has been achieved does not suggest that now is the time for relaxation. The wave of change, on whose crest our profession has ridden continues to roll forward; the future should be an infinitely more dynamic period than even the recent past. The next half century presents, perhaps, the greatest challenge that the profession has ever faced.

In order to meet our responsibilities in such a world we must make a concerted effort to foresee changes in the environment which will affect the profession. We must then analyze and prepare for the professional opportunities arising from these changes and for the problems created by them.

The monetary policies of governments concerning the supply of currency and credit have a marked influence on the economic activity and level of prices within the respective countries and on the currency exchange rates between countries. In spite of the encouraging efforts toward stabilization in many countries, there seems to be at least a moderate long-range inflationary trend in most countries and in a few of them the problem is serious right now.

We are experiencing a marked increase in international investment in productive facilities and a growing trade in consumer goods. The free flow of funds on an international level, faster and better travel and communication facilities, closer financial, political and industrial contacts among nations—all these factors help to increase this trend. International trade and investment seem destined to expand.

Rapid technological advances are also changing our economic and professional environment. Some of these advances result in new products which are stimulating consumer demand, and the related increase in productive and marketing effort is raising the general level of economic activity. Other advances are being made in productive facilities and industrial efficiency. Industrial automation through the use of electronic data processing and control equipment is a notable example of this trend.

Accompanying these technological and other economic changes are trends toward expansion in large corporations and the growth of small businesses. This simultaneous growth at both ends of the business spectrum is making an important contribution to the flexibility and soundness of the economy.

An important effect of these trends will be a general increase in the need for all of the services presently rendered by accountants and probably a demand for new services. It is conceivable that the public may look to us to extend our attest function to the area of management performance generally. Constructive tax planning for clients is becoming increasingly important, and I think it is clear that this trend will continue at an accelerated pace. No one has better opportunities than accountants to observe the overall impact of specific tax provisions on a wide variety of business transactions. Consequently, in addition to their concern with the effect on particular taxpayers, they are in an excellent position to evaluate the implications for the economy as a whole. Their participation in the formulation of tax policy and administration is not only an opportunity, but must now be considered an obligation.

The role of people trained in accounting will become very important on study commissions of federal, state and local governments. We should welcome the chance for accountants to render service in planning and projecting public programs such as transit systems, social welfare plans, educational facilities and the like.

Management services are a natural outgrowth of competent audit service. In the performance of an audit the accountant obtains a thorough understanding of a company's organizational structure, management, internal control, and of its problems and plans. The challenge to the accountant of the future in expanding his management advisory services lies in the recognition of the many management problems, and in applying to their solution not only the techniques with which he has long been familiar, but also those involving mathematical and electronic data processing applications and other techniques that have received increasing attention in recent years. This, however, does not represent any revolution in the field of accounting. It is the natural evolution of an alert profession responding to the needs of a dynamic society. The origin of our Firm dates back to the engagement of our co-founders—Charles Waldo Haskins and Elijah Watt Sells—to reorganize the accounting system of the United States Government.

There are a number of problems that are concomitant with our opportunities.

At this stage in our history, despite great strides made by the profession in many areas, there remains a lack of knowledge and understanding on the part of the public—even large segments of the business world—concerning the nature of our practice. Ownership of securities will be more widespread as personal incomes increase and more funds are available to invest and, therefore, the group of people interested in corporate reports will be larger. As a profession, we must work to bring about a better public understanding of our responsibilities and eliminate some annoying popular misconceptions.

Effective improvement in the public's concept of our profession requires more than skill in interpreting the meaning of accounting. We need to move forward on a broader front by accepting social responsibility and demonstrating a sense of obligation to the public to a greater extent than we do now. If people recognize that accountants both as professionals and as citizens are concerned with the good of society as a whole, they will do so because accountancy has shown the public how the profession works for the general welfare. This is the message enunciated by Charles Waldo Haskins seventy years ago.

Competence is the hallmark of any profession. A high level of competence has been achieved and maintained by public accountants in the past and this is one of the reasons for the profession's spectacular growth and promising future. We should be cautious, however, not to jeopardize our future prospects by failing to recognize realistic boundaries of our areas of competence. It is important that we recognize that certain specialized areas are beyond the competence of some, or perhaps all, accountants.

Research is the door that will open the way to progress. Lest we feel apologetic about the persistence of perplexing unsolved problems, I think we should recognize that they are not an indication of dilatory action in the past, but that on the contrary, they arise largely from changing conditions and the increasing complexity of business operations. We must pursue our quest for solutions. As an example, the apparent long-range inflationary trend in most countries emphasizes the need for further study of statements prepared on a price-level basis showing the effect of significant changes in the purchasing power of the currency in which the business is conducted. Considerable study has been devoted to this subject but more is needed.

We must also realize that accounting research can only act as an instrument of guidance, not one of force, and that the validity of accounting principles must be demonstrated by their practical usefulness. We should bear in mind that theory which cannot stand the acid test of practice is not good theory, and that practice which is not compatible with sound logic and reasoning is not good practice. Furthermore, accounting research is incomplete unless it can be channeled into improved understanding of financial statements by those who use them. Criticism of accounting principles in the past has sometimes resulted from failures of understanding rather than from the principles themselves.

Further study and improvement of auditing standards and procedures is another major problem confronting future accountants. It vitally affects the economics of our practice, our legal responsiiblities, and the public's confidence in our services. Progress has been made in the development of statistical sampling as a means of measuring the extent of uncertainty in tests based on an evaluation of internal control and in the development of our Auditape system for retrieving and controlling information in computer systems. This is only a beginning, however, and much remains to be done.

The accountant of the future will require an educational program which will include more liberal education—education that enlarges the mind, that enables him to recognize new problems and generate new solutions. He should learn more about the history of our society, the part played by the individual in society, and the part that great ideas have played in the foundation of contemporary civilization. This means great literature and history and sociology and political science—the subjects with which too often accountants find they are deficient in comparison to client executives with whom they discuss important matters. At the same time, his program will require greatly increased technical knowledge to enable him to cope with the demands of more sophisticated management problems.

It will be a continuing responsibility of future accountants to watch for changes in their environment or professional practice which might require adaptation, clarification, or extension of their codes of ethics. The standing of the profession today is based largely on its reputation for independence, and the future depends on continuing to earn it.

Future accountants must also recognize their interdependence on each other. Each has an obligation to his contemporaries in matters pertaining to competence, independence, and participation in civic and professional affairs. Any accountant who undertakes engagements for which he lacks competence, who breaches the standards of ethics or independence, or who conducts his practice solely out of self-interest without regard to the public interest, will do irreparable harm to the profession. The effect of the actions of each accountant of the future, as well as those of today, ordinarily will be either positive or negative.

The accounting profession has achieved general recognition and great stature, but it is merely on the threshold of its greatest era of contribution and achievement. Social, political, and economic trends as well as the complexity of business organizations have made knowledge of accounting an absolute essential of top management. Many top executives, without an accounting background, feel isolated because of that situation. The accountant of tomorrow can bridge that gap. In addition to his services in the attest, tax, and management services areas he has an obligation to become a frank and confidential adviser to chief executives to provide the understanding of accounting intricacies necessary to successful operation of a business. In many instances he is the only objective sounding board available to the chief executive and he must make himself available for that purpose.

New forces are at work in the world and are gaining momentum from vastly increased communications capability which make it imperative that we develop a world outlook. Such a world outlook recognizes the simple fact that no one country can be superior in all resources, particularly in that most important resource of all, the intellect. A given country presently may have a less advanced technology than another, but it does not follow that the brainpower of its leading thinkers is proportionately less. Thus, the challenge we face is to bring minds together in that two-way process in which each party learns from the other, and both gain. This means that we must take ideas on their merits regardless of source, seeking substance and meaning before practical implementation. Without a world outlook, we may fail to perceive a better way of doing things because all of us find it difficult to change our habitual home-grown viewpoints achieved by long, hard but often insulated thought.

The problems I have discussed are not the only heritage of the future accountant. He will be the beneficiary of the impressive record of progress of our Firm and profession to date, which provides a formidable base for attacking these problems. He inherits challenging opportunities for service in a dynamic world.

This history of our Firm is but a prologue to a record of greater achievement which will be written in the future based on a firm knit together in cooperation and cohesiveness with a common effort, a common sense of purpose, and a common tradition.

17

The New Decade

On May 31, 1970 John W. Queenan retired as Managing Partner and was succeeded by Michael N. Chetkovich. The managing partners of the Firm had come from the east and the middle west: New York, Iowa, Illinois, and Kansas. Completing the sweep of the Country, the new Managing Partner is from California, where his education was at the University of California, with a B.A. (1939) and an M.S. (1940), and with membership in the honorary business fraternity of Beta Gamma Sigma (where in his senior year he was president), and Beta Alpha Psi, the accounting fraternity. He was elected to Phi Beta Kappa at Berkeley in 1939.

On graduating in 1940 he joined McLaren, Goode, West & Co. in San Francisco.

In 1942, Mr. Chetkovich was awarded the Forbes medal of the California Society of Certified Public Accountants for the highest grade in the State on the CPA examination.

The same year he went on active duty with the United States Naval Reserve. The Navy taught him Japanese—he already spoke Croatian, the language of his parents—and assigned him to Intelligence, where he interrogated prisoners of war and translated documents. He was a lieutenant at the time of his discharge in 1946.

He returned to the staff of McLaren, Goode, West & Co., where he became a partner in 1950, and then later took an active part in professional accounting societies. He has served on many standing committees of the California CPA Society and its San Francisco Chapter, and has been chairman of several. He was a director of the state organization from 1962-64, and a vice president in 1965-66.

Michael N. Chetkovich, managing partner, who will have the opportunity and privilege of guiding Haskins & Sells in the decade of the Seventies.

In 1955, the Journal of Accountancy published his paper "Standards of Disclosure and Their Development."

Besides his professional activities, Mr. Chetkovich has taught accounting for the University of California Extension Division, and participated in community activities, including serving on the Santa Clara County grand jury in 1963 and on a lay advisory committee on a new mathematics program for the Palo Alto schools in 1964.

On the merger of McLaren, Goode, West & Co. and Haskins & Sells in 1952 he became a partner of Haskins & Sells, with N. Loyall McLaren as the senior partner in San Francisco. In 1958 on Mr. McLaren's retirement, James A. Runser (also formerly of McLaren, Goode, West & Co.) became the senior partner in San Francisco and on his retirement in 1965, Mr. Chetkovich succeeded as the senior partner in San Francisco. For a number of years it had seemed desirable to have him come to the Executive Office, but it was not until June 1, 1967 that it was possible to arrange this. At that time, he came to assist Mr. Queenan in administration.

While in San Francisco, one of the engagements under his supervision was Aramco in the course of which he spent considerable time in Saudi Arabia. On coming to New York he undertook the supervision of the General Motors engagement, and in 1968 and 1969 he visited the General Motors plants and the offices of Deloitte, Plender, Haskins & Sells and affiliates in South America, Europe, Australia, New Zealand, Africa, and the Far East.

As an enthusiastic supporter of his alma mater, he is a member of the California Alumni Association, the Golden C Club, and the Campanile Club, and is president of the New York Area alumni group. In 1967, a faculty committee of the Schools of Business gave the first "outstanding accounting alumnus of the year" award to Mr. Chetkovich. He was cited for his service to the schools and his "personal achievement as an accountant."

With the solid background of the Firm as set forth in this history and the prospects for the future as outlined by Mr. Queenan in Chapter 16, Mr. Chetkovich will have the opportunity and the privilege of guiding Haskins & Sells in the decade of the Seventies.

Appendices

Appendix A Partners and Directors of Haskins & Sells 1895—1970

Partner	Became Partner	D–Died R–Resigned
Charles W. Haskins	1895	D 1903
Elijah W. Sells	1895	D 1924
Charles S. Ludlam	1903	D 1934
Homer A. Dunn	1907	D 1935
DeRoy S. Fero	1907	R 1912
T. Finley Wharton	1907	R 1911
Howard B. Cook	1910	D 1954
Charles E. Morris	1910	D 1949
Arthur S. Vaughan	1910	D 1949
Dudley C. Morris	1910	R 1912
John F. Forbes	1912	R 1932
Leslie N. Simson	1912	R 1921
Edward Fuller	1913	D 1958
John N. Patton	1913	R 1921
Peter White	1913	D 1914
William H. Bell	1918	D 1961
Edmund C. Gause	1918	D 1961
William P. Bickett	1918	D 1938
Clifford E. Scoville	1918	D 1938
John R. Wildman	1918	D 1938
George M. Dallas	1921	R 1931
J. Harvey O'Connell	1920	D 1957
Thomas N. Willins	1921	D 1935
Edward A. Kracke	1921	D 1960
Arthur H. Carter	1922	D 1965
Charles C. Croggon	1922	
Frederick F. Hahn	1922	D 1961
Thomas H. Lawrence	1922	D 1948
Page Lawrence	1922	R 1923
Ralph T. Hollis	1922	D 1922
Frederic A. Tilton	1922	D 1942
T. L. Whitford Porte	1922	R 1925
George W. Rossetter	1922	R 1930
Arthur B. Foye	1923	
Austin R. Porterfield	1923	D 1961
Henry W. Jumonville	1923	D 1943
Edward B. McGuinn	1925	D 1952
Leslie E. Palmer	1926	D 1964
Raymond C. Reik	1926	D 1963
J. Adrian Padon	1926	R 1946
Franklin Bowman	1928	D 1961
W. Melville Coursen	1928	D 1961
Arthur M. Lovibond	1928	D 1962
J. Frank Pflug	1928	D 1938
Palen P. Rossman	1928	D 1953
Charles R. Bowen	1929	D 1959

Cyril N. Bullock	1929	D 1944
Lloyd L. Tompkins	1929	D 1954
Archibald F. Wagner	1929	D 1969
George P. Auld	1930	D 1962
Pearce C. Davis	1930	R 1942
Thomas V. Barb	1931	D 1969
Orion N. Hutchinson	1931	
Milon M. Stone	1931	D 1955
Henry W. Welsch	1931	R 1938
Percy R. Everett	1932	D 1969
Aubrey C. Fullerton	1932	D 1963
Andrew Stewart	1932	
Paul W. Pinkerton	1932	D 1940
Spencer B. Stevenson	1932	R 1942
Judson E. Krueger	1932	R 1934
H. Brooks Davies	1933	D 1958
Frederick C. Rohwerder	1933	D 1950
William M. Trant	1933	R 1935
James M. Cashin	1934	
Henry W. Goodson	1934	
James K. Gregory	1934	D 1953
J. Wilbur Haines	1934	D 1967
John M. Neumayer	1934	
Ralph W. Peters	1934	
Weldon Powell	1934	D 1965
James Clarke	1934	R 1942
Gordon M. Hill	1935	
Murdock N. MacRae	1936	D 1955
Vernon Thompson	1936	
George E. Conroy	1937	
John L. McConn	1937	R 1942
Raymond E. North	1937	R 1946
Harold W. Scott	1937	D 1965
Charles W. Swormstedt	1937	D 1962
Fletcher O. Johnson	1938	R 1950
Emil F. Bohne	1939	
Fred P. Carleton	1939	D 1952
Harry L. Erb	1939	
John W. Queenan	1939	
Everett J. Shifflett	1939	
J. Harry Williams	1939	
William J. Fronk	1940	D 1962
Paul K. Webster	1940	D 1957
Edmund A. Clarke	1941	
George M. Hayward	1941	R 1948
Casper B. Apple	1942	D 1966
Frank J. Donohue	1942	D 1960
H. Ashlin Dykes	1942	R 1970
Robert L. Reamy	1942	
Lester S. Davis	1942	
Earle M. Williams	1942	R 1943
Berthold Luedemann	1942	D 1943
Walter J. Harrison	1943	D 1952
Joel Hunter, Jr.	1943	R 1951
Ralph S. Johns	1943	
Loy J. Lucia	1943	R 1954
Otto Pelzer	1943	R 1945
J. L. Pflug	1943	R 1946
L. Joseph Case	1944	
Frank E. Gray	1944	D 1962
Vincent M. Kelly	1944	R 1954
Arthur W. Koelbel	1944	D 1966
A. Chester Livengood	1944	
Malcolm M. Devore	1945	
Andrew B. Fielding	1945	
Alvan B. Richardson	1945	
Arthur E. Schwertfeger	1945	
William D. Shay	1945	
Elmer G. Beamer	1946	
Rudolph J. Englert	1946	
Richard H. Grosse	1946	
Harry R. Weyrich	1946	
Paul L. Wilton	1946	
Jerome A. Benning	1947	
Lindsay R. Boyle	1947	
Samuel E. Ellis	1947	
Bertram E. Gill	1947	
Karl A. Herrhammer	1947	
Porter M. Larson	1947	
Glenn P. Leonard	1947	
Curtis H. Cadenhead	1948	
Edward L. Carey	1948	
Kay J. Jennell	1948	
Fitzroy D. Maclean	1948	
William F. Royer	1948	D 1958
John S. Schumann	1948	
William B. Tittsworth	1948	
John H. Baum	1949	D 1964
Frank G. Connelly	1949	
G. William Graham	1949	
Forest A. Klumph	1949	
Robert C. Lanka	1949	
Frank N. McClelland	1949	
George E. Babylon	1950	
Olen W. Christopherson	1950	D 1964
Burgess F. Geib	1950	
Charles F. Reinhardt	1950	
J. Edward Robertson	1950	
Curtis E. Youngdahl	1950	
Henry S. Chapin	1951	
Benton C. Coit	1951	
Presley S. Ford	1951	
Mahlon H. Grant	1951	
Thomas B. Hogan	1951	
Harold V. Petrillo	1951	
Robert H. Willson	1951	D 1955
E. Robert Billings	1952	
Gayle L. Dalferes	1952	
Henry W. Forbes	1952	R 1970
Gordon C. Stubbs	1952	
Russell D. Tipton	1952	
N. Loyall McLaren	1952	

John W. Boulter	1952	D 1964	Ervin A. Stadler	1955	
Michael N. Chetkovich	1952		Gustave A. Reh, Jr.	1955	
John H. Davis	1952	R 1958	Charles C. Gabrielson	1956	
Emmett S. Harrington	1952		Virgil F. Blank	1956	
Lewis Lilly	1952	D 1954	Richard S. Drake	1956	
Frederick W. Lyon	1952	D 1970	E. Jonathan Harvey	1956	
A. Thomas Murphy	1952		Charles F. Lemons	1956	
David J. W. Patrick	1952	D 1969	Louis A. MacKenzie	1956	
James A. Runser	1952		Gordon L. Murray	1956	
James A. Tannahill	1952		Paul W. Pinkerton	1956	
Arthur A. Wender	1952		Charles W. Wilkins	1956	
John F. West	1952		James A. Wilson	1956	
Rodney D. White	1952	D 1964	Glenn O. Williams	1956	
Charles N. Whitehead	1952		Charles L. Clapp	1956	
Lorin H. Wilson	1952		Colin Park	1956	
Sir Russell Kettle	1952	D 1968	Edward E. Hunter	1956	D 1963
Sir Alan Rae Smith	1952	D 1961	E. Leigh Bliss	1956	D 1963
James Anderson	1952		Stanley C. Goodsill	1956	
George Cochrane	1952	D 1967	Ian K. Lamberton	1956	
E. Kenneth Ernest	1952		N. John Pasch	1956	
William Eyre	1952	D 1954	Stanley Rosch	1956	R 1965
William S. McNamara	1952		Robert T. M. McPhail	1956	
John F. Parnaby	1952	R 1959	Wilbur R. Irwin	1956	D 1962
Oliver W. Seifert	1952	R 1964	Jacob H. Imig	1956	
Paul Mestern	1953		Robert W. Johnson	1956	
Karl R. Zimmermann	1953		Joseph T. Sullivan	1956	
Thomas J. Graves	1953		James J. Scarborough	1956	
Robert G. Koeppel	1953		Edward L. Powers	1956	
Chauncey A. Norton	1953		Douglas G. Cochrane	1957	
Ferdinand M. Pitner	1953		Joe L. Hagman	1957	
Homer A. Sayad	1953		Maurice S. Newman	1957	
Ralph B. Stratford	1954	D 1962	Julius W. Phoenix, Jr.	1957	
Harry C. Visse	1954		William J. Planthaber	1957	
Albert J. Henke	1954		William K. Quinlan	1957	
Glen R. McDaniel	1954		Walter A. Ruschmeyer	1957	
Bernard W. Arvin	1954		Russell P. Shomler	1957	
Richard B. Keigley	1954		William J. Sturm	1957	
Ross C. Kingsbury	1954	D 1962	William C. Witler	1957	
Philip J. Sandmaier, Jr.	1954		William L. Schnatterly	1957	
J. William Stewart, Jr.	1954		Ralph S. Dobbins	1958	
George F. Reuter	1954	D 1967	C. Howard Kast	1958	
Paul H. Crandall	1954	D 1966	Eugene L. Larkin, Jr.	1958	
Gordon L. Hopper	1954		Sherman L. Lewis	1958	R 1964
Howard R. Reuter	1954		Jack Macy	1958	R 1969
Edward W. Carmody	1954		Robert L. Steele	1958	
W. Guy Densem	1955		Robert C. Tatgenhorst	1958	
Frank X. Fields	1955		William D. Gasser	1958	R 1967
Oscar S. Gellein	1955		Roland E. King	1959	
Leo W. Hesselman, Jr.	1955		D. Robert Nicholson	1959	
John C. McCormick	1955		Samuel Rees III	1959	
Lad A. Rehula	1955		Henry J. Sebastian	1959	
Philip J. Schuele	1955		Kenneth W. Stringer	1959	
Lawrence M. Walsh	1955		Robert E. Whyte	1959	
William A. Waymouth	1955		Richard G. Williams	1959	
Daniel M. Sheehan	1955	D 1967	Robert G. Wright	1959	
James R. Favret	1955		Lynn E. Baxter	1959	

Z. Vernon Derrick	1959	
Donald A. Miller	1959	
Henry R. Nelson	1959	R 1969
Fred M. Oliver	1959	
Max A. Millett	1959	
G. Wesley Johnson	1959	R 1964
Delford W. Edens	1960	
John A. Gidney	1960	R 1962
Thomas W. Hudson, Jr.	1960	
Sigvart O. Joraanstad	1960	
Norman R. Kerth	1960	
Virgil V. Pedersen	1960	
Wilbert H. Schwotzer	1960	
Ralph P. Simpson	1960	
J. Gilbert Tinker	1960	
George K. Palmer	1960	R 1964
Milton J. Urner	1960	
Joseph Dranguet	1960	
Guy Myrph Foote	1960	
Ralph T. Bartlett	1961	
Robert C. Dickey	1961	
Laurence O. Eames	1961	
Martin M. Friedman	1961	
Allan A. Gilman	1961	
Arthur P. Metzger	1961	
John E. Skrifvars	1961	
C. Keith Stott	1961	
Carl L. Sturgis	1961	
Charles A. Trice	1961	
William Wright	1961	
Hugh F. Purvis	1961	
James I. Keller	1961	
Clayton L. Bullock	1961	
Lyndon C. Conlon	1961	
Walter P. Davison	1961	
Conrad G. Demro, Jr.	1961	
Earl L. Henrichs	1961	
E. Nolan Johnson	1961	R 1970
Allen Tomlinson	1961	
Kenneth D. Walker	1961	D 1965
William R. Wright	1961	R 1964
Thomas E. Stanley	1961	D 1964
Axel C. Ahlberg	1961	
Lawrence D. Wilch	1961	R 1962
Mack H. Barnes, Sr.	1961	
Walter C. Askew, Jr.	1961	D 1968
Mack H. Barnes, Jr.	1961	
William A. Mills	1961	
D. Wayne Ashby, Jr.	1961	
Loyd F. Armstrong	1962	
Oreson H. Christensen	1962	
Howard L. Henning	1962	
John C. McCarthy	1962	
William T. Miller	1962	R 1968
Frank H. Tiedemann	1962	
Kennard W. Webster	1962	

Russell W. Wende	1962	
Charles S. Rockey	1962	
Robert Caldwell	1962	
Russell L. Campbell	1962	
William Craemer, Jr.	1962	
Lawrence J. Klauder	1962	D 1966
David E. Longacre, Jr.	1962	
John H. Prentice	1962	
Nicholas J. Raftery	1962	R 1964
H. Edward Slough	1962	R 1966
Sydney V. Young	1962	
Harold E. Amsler	1962	
Philip F. Stafford	1962	R 1967
Lester Wichterman	1962	D 1966
Morris L. Crouse	1963	D 1965
George A. DeBon, Jr.	1963	
Fernando J. Domenich	1963	
James A. Gallagher	1963	
E. Frederick Halstead	1963	
John E. Kolesar	1963	
Donald L. Krier	1963	
Edward R. Lang	1963	
Don A. Nelson	1963	
Haldon G. Robinson	1963	
Robert F. Skeehan	1963	
Charles G. Steele	1963	
Leo C. Voet	1963	
Carroll L. Webb, Jr.	1963	
George K. Watson	1963	
Harold J. Watson	1963	
N. Edward Drayer	1963	
Clarence E. Edwards	1963	
John B. Moore	1963	
Paul K. Gotwald	1963	
H. Oscar Zimmerman	1963	
Jay A. Phillips	1963	
Harry D. Hopson	1963	
Sidney M. Lewis	1963	
Homer L. Luther	1963	
Jesse W. Martin	1963	
Gregg C. Waddill	1963	
Julian A. Hawk	1963	
Charles F. Collins	1963	
Robert E. Hadeler	1963	
Charles A. Perkins	1963	
Henry Wagner, Jr.	1963	
Edgar J. Bostick	1964	
Lawrence F. Chandler	1964	
John M. Crawford	1964	
Robert J. Fawls	1964	D 1970
John W. Gilbert	1964	
Allen B. Hatfield	1964	
Thomas M. Kupfer	1964	
Roy P. Lund	1964	R 1970
Murdock M. MacRae, Jr.	1964	R 1970
Lloyd S. Mosher	1964	

Kenneth R. Swanson	1964	
Robert B. Van Arsdale	1964	
Arthur F. Wilkins	1964	
Wayne Williamson	1964	
Edward S. Culver	1964	
Norman E. Jones	1964	
William S. Cobb	1965	
Lynd E. Cohick	1965	
Bruce L. Davis, Jr.	1965	
John T. Farrell, Jr.	1965	
James O. Funderburk	1965	
Howard H. Hankins	1965	
Walter H. Hanshaw	1965	
Joseph P. Healy	1965	
Terence F. Healy	1965	
William B. LaPlace	1965	
Vernon L. Libby	1965	
William B. Mansfield	1965	
Robert D. Niemeyer	1965	
Jerome D. Solari	1965	
Charles R. Talley	1965	
DeWitt C. Warren	1965	
Curtis H. Cadenhead, Jr.	1966	
Robert J. Cisneros	1966	
Camillus D. Conway	1966	
William W. Cope	1966	
Adrian F. Cummings	1966	
Edward R. Deppman	1966	
William S. Easton	1966	
Jack L. Elliott	1966	
John A. Favret	1966	
Hugh A. Garnett	1966	
William W. Gerecke	1966	
Wilbur D. Harris	1966	
Edward J. Lill	1966	
Robert L. Potter	1966	
Warren K. Reed	1966	
Raymond D. Spinola	1966	
Frederick A. Zimmer	1966	
Virgil S. Tilly, Sr.	1967	D 1969
E. C. Leonard	1967	
Ralph D. Bowen	1967	
Claude T. Scott	1967	
Virgil S. Tilly, Jr.	1967	
Michael L. Balint	1967	
Jack E. Brooks	1967	
Eugene H. Cobaugh	1967	
Edward N. Darcey	1967	
Albert B. Dean	1967	
Hugh M. Eggan	1967	
Joseph E. Elmlinger	1967	
William O. Hetts	1967	
Reynard H. Hoffman	1967	
Donald R. Johnson	1967	
Sven E. V. Johnson	1967	
John F. McDonnell	1967	
Neil F. O'Connell	1967	
Edward A. Shaffer	1967	
Frank H. Spearman III	1967	
Kenneth E. Staples	1967	
Kenneth E. Studdard	1967	
Albert W. White, Jr.	1967	
Gerard A. Zulli	1967	
Dale D. Baker	1968	
Frank J. Borelli	1968	
Dwight Brown	1968	
John C. Crane	1968	
Richard F. Crilly	1968	
Robert J. Cruikshank	1968	
Henry D. Forer	1968	
Raymond L. Gibbs	1968	
Jerry W. Kolb	1968	
Burnell L. Larson	1968	
Richard V. Leighton	1968	
James B. Miller	1968	
Daniel J. Moylan	1968	
Olney F. Otto	1968	
Lowell S. Pethley	1968	
Sheldon Richman	1968	
George H. Rowe	1968	
Irwin C. Rust	1968	
Roy J. Spaulding	1968	
Francis J. Thomason	1968	
Thomas R. Warner	1968	
Hardy T. Williamson	1968	
John F. Utley	1968	
Francis W. Ascher	1969	
Francois R. Barfuss	1969	
Frederick W. Bassinger	1969	
Albert J. Bova	1969	
A. Grant Bowen	1969	
Clyde F. Brennan	1969	
Leonard M. Brooke	1969	
Robert W. Buesser	1969	
Robert B. Caballero	1969	
H. Clayton Chandler	1969	
Kenneth C. Cole, Jr.	1969	
Harold J. Corwin	1969	
James F. Dunn, Jr.	1969	
August Glissmeyer, Jr.	1969	
Robert S. Gorab	1969	
Kostas Gussis	1969	
Harry O. Hempy, Jr.	1969	
Dean M. Johnston	1969	
Ernest H. Kenyon	1969	
Allan A. Leiter	1969	
James L. McGregor	1969	
Eugene W. Morgerson	1969	
Thomas S. Oehring	1969	
Harold K. Robertson	1969	
Bennett S. Robinson	1969	
Millard E. Smith	1969	

Robert G. Speidel	1969
Armin C. Tufer	1969
John F. Walsh	1969
Robert D. Walter	1969
Charles A. Walworth	1969
Warren K. Wentworth, Jr.	1969
Gary R. West	1969
Robert D. Arnett	1969
J. Edward Sinclair	1969
Gene R. Mendel	1969
Francisco Arabia	1969
Ralph J. Kliber	1969
Cletus J. Welling	1969
Charles V. Collins	1969
Robert W. Duffield	1969
Norbert T. Madison	1969
Thomas H. Wright	1969
Alphonse R. Staeger	1969
Linn A. Walter	1969
Robert L. Sanford	1969
Patrick J. Freeman	1969
Robert B. Zettel	1969
George C. Ball	1969
Robert H. Bauman	1969 R 1970
Miller Montag	1970
Stanley H. Malis	1970
John J. McIsaac, Sr.	1970
Lewis M. Foster	1970
D. Harold Sullivan	1970
Madison D. Kimball	1970
Claude R. LaPlante	1970
Anthony J. Billie	1970
Robert D. Diggins	1970
Harry D. Baker	1970
Charles R. Ballard	1970
Stanley R. Brekhus	1970
Frank A. Bruni	1970
Joseph Calace-Mottola	1970
Albert A. Cardone	1970
Milton C. Clow	1970
Harold J. Coltman	1970
Ronald L. Colwell	1970
James W. Craft	1970
R. Dougal Crowe	1970
William M. Flansburg	1970
Robert J. Fuchs	1970
James V. Gillick	1970
W. Robert Hampton	1970
C. Harold Hippler, Jr.	1970
Donald W. Hornburg	1970
Clarence W. Houghton	1970
Henry Jacquemet	1970
Gordon M. Johns	1970
Richard A. Johnson	1970
Harold G. Levell	1970
Edward J. McGovern	1970
Sidney Meyer	1970
David W. Moore	1970
Douglas L. Newell	1970
Ralph W. Newkirk, Jr.	1970
Costas C. Nicolaides	1970
Francis C. Oatway	1970
Gerald F. O'Neil	1970
David C. Ranney	1970
William H. Ryan	1970
Thomas J. D. Shepherd	1970
Alan Sigman	1970
Edward M. Sullivan	1970
Allan L. Swormstedt	1970
Patrick J. Waide, Jr.	1970
Martin I. Wasserman	1970
Daniel G. Weinstein	1970
Jerome L. Weinstein	1970
George Weinstein	1970
Bertram Frankenberger, Jr.	1970

Director	Became Director
Vincent T. Donnelly	1963
Leonard Pace	1963
Robert L. Kelly	1967
Richard E. Klinger	1968
Richard J. Novo	1969
Marvin C. Kelly	1970

Appendix B Meetings

1903-13	New York—for partners and managers
1914-18	No meetings due to First World War
1919	New York—25th Anniversary meeting (15 partners and 18 managers)
1920-22	New York (with a "day in the country for golf and dinner dance")
1923	New York—business sessions only due to ill health of Mr. Sells
1924-31	New York
1932	No meeting due to recession
1933-40	New York
1941-45	No meetings due to Second World War
1946-47	New York—but separate meetings for partners (64) and principals (58)

Meetings of Partners and Directors

1948-49	New York—in two groups—one in June and one in September
1950-52	Skytop Lodge, Skytop, Pennsylvania
1953	The Greenbrier, White Sulphur Springs, West Virginia for partners (131) and wives (117)
1954	Skytop Lodge
1955	Seigniory Club, Montebello, Quebec
1956	Skytop Lodge
1957	The Greenbrier for partners (191) and wives (173)
1958	The Homestead, Hot Springs, Virginia
1959	Del Monte Lodge, Pebble Beach, California
1960	Lake Placid Club, Essex County, New York
1961	The Greenbrier for partners (263) and wives (250)
1962	The Homestead
1963	Lake Placid Club
1964	The Homestead
1965	The Greenbrier for partners and directors (300) and wives (280)
1966	The Homestead
1967	Arizona Biltmore Hotel, Phoenix, Arizona
1968-69	The Homestead
1970	The Greenbrier for partners and directors and wives

Meetings of Principals and Managers

1948-52	New York
1953-55	Westchester Country Club
1956	Skytop Lodge for principals and managers (116) and wives (94)
1957-58	Westchester Country Club
1959-61	Skytop Lodge
1962	Lake Placid Club for principals and managers (235) and wives (210)
1963-66	Skytop Lodge
1967	Lake Placid Club for principals and managers (366) and wives (323)
1968	Skytop Lodge
1969	Skytop Lodge and Buck Hill Falls Inn
1970	Skytop Lodge and Buck Hill Falls Inn

Appendix C Offices

1895 New York
1900 Chicago
1901 London
1902 St. Louis
1902 Cleveland
1903 Pittsburgh
1910 Baltimore
1912 San Francisco
1915 Watertown, New York—Closed 1931
1915 Atlanta
1915 Denver
1916 Los Angeles
1917 Seattle
1917 Detroit
1918 Boston
1919 New Orleans
1919 Philadelphia
1920 Shanghai—Closed 1942
1920 Tulsa
1920 Kansas City
1920 Cincinnati
1920 Dallas
1920 Havana—Closed 1962
1920 Paris
1920 Buffalo—Closed 1934—Reopened 1955
1920 Salt Lake City—Closed 1931—Reopened 1959
1921 Portland, Oregon
1921 New York—Uptown—Closed 1954
1921 Minneapolis
1922 Newark
1923 Providence—Closed 1932—Reopened 1954
1923 San Diego—Closed 1934—Reopened 1954
1923 Birmingham—Closed 1930—Reopened 1956
1924 Berlin—Closed 1941
1925 Brooklyn—Closed 1927
1926 Charlotte
1926 Jacksonville
1926 Manila—Closed 1941
1929 Chattanooga—Closed 1932—Reopened 1965
1932 Milwaukee
1937 Houston
1939 Louisville—Closed 1949—Reopened 1962
1941 Dayton—Closed 1951—Reopened 1961
1954 Medford
1955 San Juan
1956 New Haven
1956 Omaha
1956 Honolulu
1956 Kahului, Maui

1956 Lihue, Kauai
1956 Rochester
1957 Ponce
1957 Washington
1958 Hilo
1959 Phoenix
1961 Indianapolis
1961 Columbus
1961 Savannah
1961 Miami
1961 Fort Lauderdale
1961 Orlando
1961 Leesburg—Closed 1965
1962 Allentown
1962 Wilkes-Barre
1963 Memphis
1964 Lawrence
1964 Manchester
1964 Saint Paul
1964 Tampa
1966 Greensboro
1966 Orange County
1967 Colorado Springs
1967 Fort Worth
1967 Greenville
1967 Oklahoma City
1967 Richmond
1967 Mobile
1968 Las Vegas
1968 White Plains
1968 San Jose
1969 Port Huron
1970 San Antonio
1970 Hartford
1970 Wilmington

Appendix D Mergers and Acquisitions

Date	Name	Office
1901	Conant & Grant	London
1912	John F. Forbes	San Francisco
1915	Scoville & Mullen	Watertown, New York
1916	Frederick F. Hahn	Los Angeles
1919	Henry J. Jumonville	New Orleans
1920	George R. Lamb	Cincinnati
1920	Grover C. Bland	Dallas
1920	Lawrence & Lawrence	Denver
1920	Hervey S. Champlin	Buffalo
1920	Stevenson & Carson	Shanghai
1921	Hollis, Tilton & Porte	Detroit
1921	Augustus Nickerson	Boston
1921	F. M. Weaver	Kansas City
1922	Archibald F. Wagner	Minneapolis
1923	C. Palmer Parker	Birmingham
1923	Wilfred L. Hagerty	Providence
1932	George H. Cheyne	Milwaukee
1937	Clarke & Larkin	Manila
1942	*Joel Hunter, Jr.	Atlanta
1944	*William McAdam	Seattle
1949	*Tuohy and Shepherd	Seattle
1950	*Gayle L. Dalferes	New Orleans
1951	*Estate of M. A. Preisz, Sr.	Portland, Oregon
1952	McLaren, Goode, West & Co.	Seattle, San Francisco, Los Angeles, New York
1952	Deloitte, Plender, Griffiths & Co.	New York, Boston, Chicago, Cincinnati, Los Angeles
1953	Zimmermann & Company	New York
1953	*Francis E. Welch	Boston
1954	Stratford, Visse & Company	Portland, Medford, Oregon
1954	*Jensen, Morgan & Company	Seattle
1954	Crandall & Reuter	San Diego
1955	Sparrow, Waymouth & Company	San Juan
1955	*Harry C. Northrop	Charlotte
1955	*John T. Pasquill	Portland, Oregon
1955	Rouse, Favret & Company	Cincinnati
1956	Gabrielson, O'Sullivan, Poulson & Co.	Los Angeles
1956	Williams, Clapp & Company	Rochester
1956	*Raymond V. Ellis	Rochester
1956	*W. R. Haughwont	Rochester
1956	Young, Lamberton & Pearson	Honolulu, Kahului, Lihue
1956	Irwin-Imig Company	Omaha
1956	*Estate of Jack Wright	Rochester
1956	*Richards & Patterson	Rochester
1956	Scarborough & Powers	Birmingham
1957	W. L. Schnatterly & Company	Seattle

1958	*Miller, Donaldson & Company	San Francisco
1958	Henderson, Henderson & Dobbins	Hilo
1958	Miller, Franklin, McLeod & Co.	Rochester
1958	*Walter S. MacAllister	Rochester
1958	*J. W. Jury	Omaha
1959	Johnson, Millett, Stott & Brooksby	Phoenix
1959	Wells, Baxter & Miller	Salt Lake City
1959	*H. Daniel Campbell	Omaha
1959	*David H. Risbel	Philadelphia
1960	*Bailey, Norman and Spalsbury	Phoenix
1960	Palmer and Urner	San Diego
1960	Dranguet, Foote & Company	Dallas
1961	Pentland, Purvis, Keller & Co.	Miami, Fort Lauderdale, Orlando, Leesburg
1961	Redeker, Stanley, Ahlberg & Wilch	Denver
1961	Barnes, Askew, Mills & Company	Atlanta, Savannah
1961	*Milan M. Johnson	Los Angeles
1961	D. Wayne Ashby, Jr.	Columbus
1962	Hiram E. Decker & Company	Chicago
1962	Charles S. Rockey & Company	Philadelphia, Allentown, Wilkes-Barre
1963	George K. Watson & Company	Philadelphia
1963	*R. W. B. Newkirk, Jr.	Philadelphia
1963	*Frederick W. Hesse	Atlanta
1963	Phillips, Sheffield, Hopson, Lewis & Luther	Houston
1963	Arnold, Hawk & Cuthbertson	Dayton
1964	Robert O. Douglas & Company	Boston, Lawrence, Manchester
1965	Homer K. Jones & Company	Memphis
1965	*J. H. Hardy & Associates	Chattanooga
1965	*Edith Moore	Chattanooga
1965	*Peisch & Peisch	Minneapolis
1966	*Webster McCann	Boston
1967	*F. B. Andrews & Company	Chicago
1967	W. O. Ligon & Company	Tulsa, Fort Worth
1969	Francisco A. Arabia	San Juan
1969	Milledge, Sinclair, Mendel & Co.	Houston
1969	Rutten, Welling & Company	Detroit, Cleveland, Port Huron
1970	Lewis & Montag	San Antonio
1970	Stanley H. Malis & Co.	Hartford
1970	Spark, Mann & Co.	Boston
1970	Weinstein & Timm	New Haven

**Denotes acquisitions*

Index